Nurseries AND MORE

The Complete Manual of Baby Accessory Patterns

Linda W. Storm

Photographs by Martin Greeson and John Storm

Illustrations by Lynn Schuck and Bud Schilz

WERSTORM PRESS

Springfield, Ohio

786 Westchester Park Drive
Springfield, OH 45504

Published in Springfield, Ohio 45504 by Werstorm Press

Manufactured in the United States of America
Covers by Bud Schilz

On the cover: Jesse's Room
All crib, changing table and wall items were made from fabric provided by V.I.P. Fabrics Very Important Bear collection. The red fabric and printed panel headboard were selected to stimulate and entertain Jesse while in the crib after naps. The changing table was placed next to the crib with the diaper stacker between for convenience of changing either in the crib or on the changing table. The changing table has the catch-all and stacker close at hand with all the necessitites to allow Mom to maintain control of baby during changing to avoid the possibility of the child falling. The catch-all is bright to keep Jesse's attention. The letter's can be pointed to and discussed during changes while the pockets can hold shoes, ointments, powders plus a few toys to keep him entertained.

Back Cover:
Pictured are all of the extra items which are needed and nice to have to make life a little more pleasant with baby. These items are also made from V.I.P. 's V.I.B. collection.

Jacque's room shows how the nursery items can grow with your child into a youth room. Her room is done with V.I.P. Lullaby Bunny fabric's.

ISBN: 0-934679-01-0   Plastic Comb Bind
ISBN: 0-934679-02-9   Perfect Bind

Dedicated to you .

That you may be inspired to create and design the unique one-of-a-kind nursery you have always dreamed of.

Acknowledgements

Through the support, encouragment and help of family, friends and neighbors, this book has come to be. First, I have to thank God for giving me this idea seven years ago while writing the first book. I didn't think I could write this one but after seven years and two more children here it is.

I would like to thank: my husband, John, who has put up with crazy schedules, the mess of fabric, paper and accessories everywhere. My children, Joey, Jacque and Jesse, who are my constant sources of inspiration and who have had to be so patient and understanding through this project. Lynn Schuck who did the original artwork. Bud Schilz who helped me complete the illustrations and who gave me an extra boost to see it finished. Candy Walters who has such a good listening ear. Her assistance in helping me get the right words and ideas on paper was invaluable. Sharon Matthews who not only read and re-read the patterns finding ways to make the patterns clear and understandable but also helped her daughter Lynn make the youth room accessories. Elizabeth (Bessie) Lerner who did such a wonderful job making the accessories and help refine the patterns while contributing some of her own ideas. My sister Mary Jane Weiss who has made phone calls and contacts while I was out of country. And my parents, William and Catherine Werst, who though retired have taken on new vocations maintaining a publishing company.

CONTENTS

*Denotes patterns with Grow-With-Me ideas.

BASSINET COMFORTER AND PILLOW

-2 yards 45" fabric
-quilt batting (extra loft)

Layout and Cut

A. Cut out two 20"x26" pieces for comforter, two 13"x16" pieces for pillow and seven 4"x45" strips for ruffles. Cut batting 20"x26". You may want 2 or even 3 layers of batting depending on how thick you want the comforter.

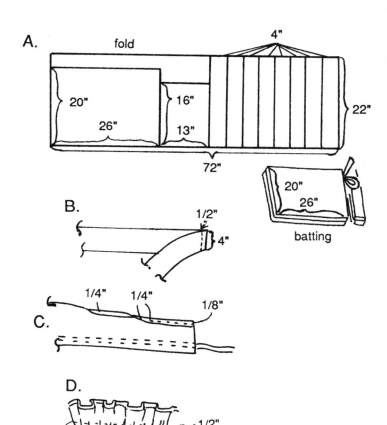

A.

batting

Sewing Directions - Comforter Ruffles

B. Place two ruffle strips right sides together, stitch 1/2" seam along 4" edge. Continue stitching strips together until four ruffle strips are joined in one strip.

C. Turn under 1/4" and 1/4" again along one edge. Stitch close to inside edge.

D. Gather opposite edge by stitching 1/4" and 1/2" from raw edge. Pull bottom threads.

Assembling

E. Pin ruffle around edges between fabric with right sides together and batting on bottom. Be sure to put extra ruffles in the corners for fullness.

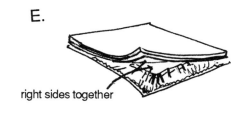

right sides together

F. Stitch 1/2" seam on three and a half sides leaving an opening in the middle of the fourth side. Clip corners and trim seams. Turn right side out. Stitch opening closed.

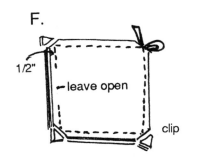

F.

1/2"

leave open

clip

1

BASSINET COMFORTER AND PILLOW
Continued

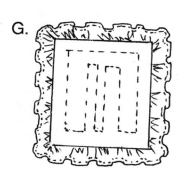

G. Pin through all layers of fabric then stitch by hand or machine every 3" or 4" to prevent the batting from slipping.

Pillow

H. Make ruffle using three 3"x45" strips. Repeat steps C and D above.

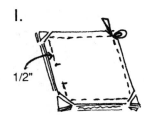

I. Take 16"x13" fabric, place right sides together. Pin ruffle in seam between fabric. Be sure to put extra ruffles in the corners for fullness. Stitch 1/2" seam on three and a half sides. Leave middle of fourth side open.

1/2"

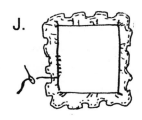

J. Turn right side out and stuff with fiberfill. Stitch seam closed.

OPTION:

Applique a design onto one side of comforter and pillow.

BASSINET HOOP CANOPY

-4 1/4 yards of 45" fabric
-one 10" or12" wood embroidery hoop
-heavy duty thread

Layout and Cut

A. Cut off 9" of fabric. From this cut two 3"x45" hanging strips.

B. Fold the four yards of fabric in half lengthwise so you will have two 2 yard pieces. Cut along fold.

Sewing Directions - Edges

C. If selvages have printing in them, press printing under and stitch close to inside edge. If selvages do not have printing in them, it is not necessary to turn them under.

D. Press under 1/2" and then 2" on both top and bottom of panel. Stitch close to inside edge.   Repeat this step for other panel.

E. Along one end of each panel, stitch 1" from outside fold. This is the top.

Hanging Strips

F. Fold 3"x45" strips in half, press. Fold edges to meet at pressed fold. Fold again on original fold so edges are in the middle. Stitch close to each edge.

G. Take one fabric strip, fold up 1" on each end. Zig zag across end through the strip making a loop.

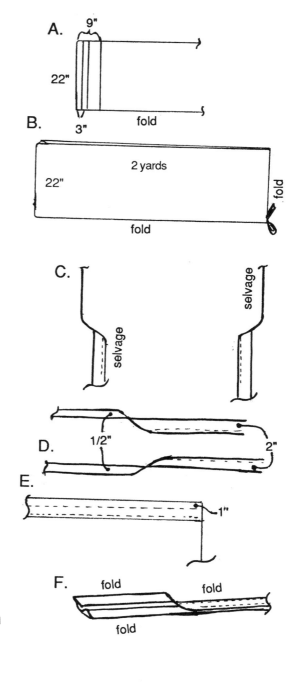

BASSINET HOOP CANOPY Continued

H. Take other hanging strip, find middle top of both canopy panels. Place one end of the hanging strip to the wrong side of the canopy panel so end of strip is 1" past bottom casing stitching. Stitch across hanging strip at each edge of casing. Repeat this step to attach other end of strip to second canopy panel.

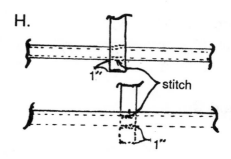
H.

Hanging

I. Insert one end of wood hoop into casing of first panel then put on one end of loop strip (so loop is toward the inside).

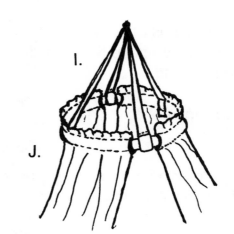
I.

J.

J. Put on second panel and other end loop strip. Close hoop with screw.

K. Pull strips together at the top so center points of strips meet. Stitch together so they are at 90' angles. Stitch along edges of top strip.

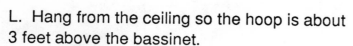
K.

L. Hang from the ceiling so the hoop is about 3 feet above the bassinet.

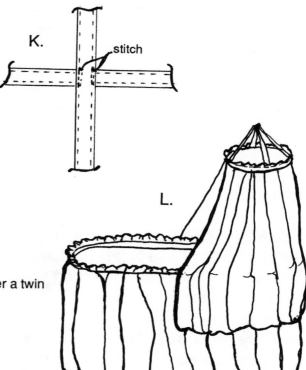
L.

Grow-With-Me Idea:

Use now over the bassinet, later over the crib and then over a twin bed.

4

BASSINET SHEET

-3/4 yard 45" fabric
-1 yard 1/4" wide elastic

NOTE: This fits 33"x17"x2" pad. It is a versatile cover for a changing table pad cover and infant seat cover.

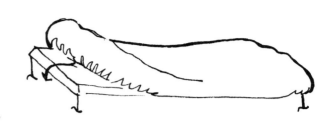

Layout and Cut

A. Cut the faric to 40"x24".

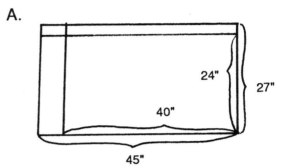

A.

Marking

B. Measure 3 1/2" both directions from each corner. Fold to match 3 1/2" marks. Measure 3 1/2" across fabric to fold. Mark.

B.

Sewing Directions - Corners

C. Stitch from 3 1/2" mark on edge to mark on fold. Clip corners 1/2" from stitching. Zig zag cut edge.

C.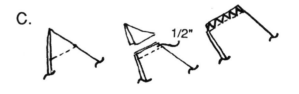

Edges

D. Turn under 1/4" and 1/4" again on all sides. Stitch close to turned under edge.

D.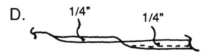

Ends

E. Cut two 11" pieces of elastic. Mark the center of each piece. Mark the center of each end of the sheet. Match the center of the elastic to the center end of the sheet. Pin. Pin ends of the elastic 2" past each corner.

E.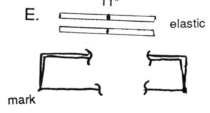

F. Stitch elastic on turned under fabric stretching it as needed.

F.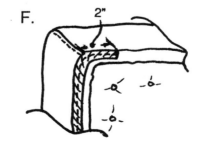

G. Repeat steps E and F for other end of sheet.

G.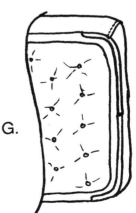

5

BASSINET SKIRT AND LINER

-5 1/4 yards of 45" fabric
-7'2" of 1/2" wide elastic
NOTE: This skirt and liner are designed to fit a bassinet
that is 26" tall with inside measurements of 86" around
top inside edge, 74" around bottom inside edge and
11 1/2" inside height.

Layout and Cut -
Skirt

A. Cut four panels 45"x33" long. Substitute
your measurements if they differ.

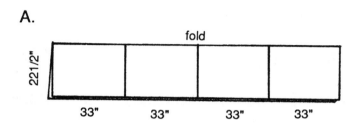

Bottom

B. Fold in half so selvages are together. On
fold of fabric, measure 28" from one cut
edge. Measure in 6 1/2" from fold on cut
edge, and at 28" mark, mark both points.
Connect marks.

Side Panel

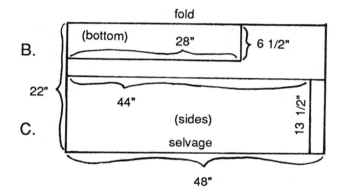

C. Along selvage, measure 44" from one cut
edge, mark. Measure 13 1/2" from selvage
toward fold on cut edge, at 44" selvage
mark, and midway between the two points.
Connect marks. Cut out the pieces along
marked lines.

D. Along 44" edge, measure 3" from each
corner. Draw a line from 3" mark to corner
on opposite side. Cut along the line.

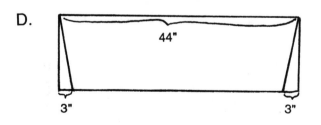

Sewing Directions -
Liner

E. Place side panels with right sides
together. Stitch 1/2" seams. Zig zag edges.

F. Press under 1/4" and 1/4" again on top of
panels. Stitch close to inside edge.

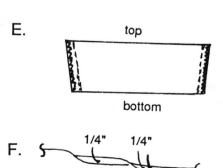

BASSINET SKIRT AND LINER Continued

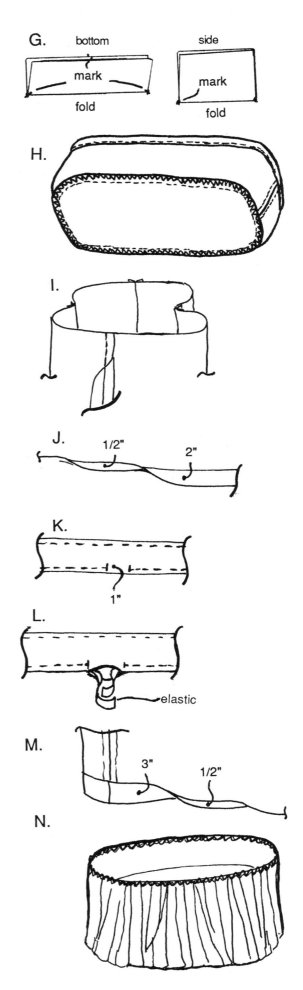

G. Fold bottom of liner and mark center of all four sides. Fold side panel and mark center of one side.

H. Place seams of liner so they match the folds of bottom panel ends. Ease side panels to the bottom panel matching center of bottom panel to center of side panel. Stitch 1/2" seam. Zig zag edges around bottom.

Sewing Directions - Skirt

I. Take two skirt panels at a time, place right sides together so selvages meet. Stitch 1/2" seam on 33" side. Press seams open. Repeat until all panels are connected in one continuous strip.

J. After all panels are joined, press under 1/2" at top of skirt. Press under 2" more.

K. Stitch close to inside edge leaving 1" open to put elastic through. Stitch close to outside edge.

L. Pull elastic through top of skirt casing. Stitch 1" opening closed.

Hem

M. Press under 1/2" then 3" at bottom of skirt. Turn up 3" for hem. Stitch by hand, machine blind hem or topstitch on machine.

Joining Skirt and Liner

N. Place bassinet liner in basket. Place skirt around the basket. Hand stitch basket liner to skirt. (Basket handles should be under the skirt.)

BATH TOY BAG

-5/8 yard 45" fabric
-1 regular size hanger

Layout and Mark

A. Cut fabric to 45"x17". Fold over 8" on one selvage. From one cut edge, measure 1", 8 3/4", 9 1/4" and 17" on top fold. Mark each point.

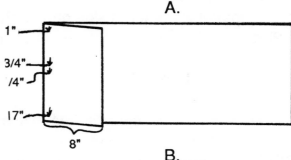

A.

B. Measure and mark 4" from 1" and 17" marks on fold. Measure 23" from top fold on cut edges, mark.

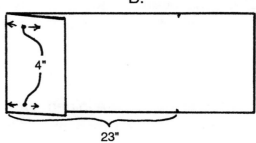

B.

Sewing Directions

C. Turn under 1/4" and 1/4" again on both ends, At center marks on top fold (8 3/4" and 9 1/4" marks) make a 1/2" buttonhole between them.

C.

D. Fold right sides together so buttonhole is on top fold. Stitch straight lines from edge of buttonhole to 4" mark at side edges; continue stitching 1/2" seam to finished edge. Cut 1/2" from stitching line. Zig zag edge.

D.

E. Fold bottom up at 23" marks. (If desired, applique a design or name on the front of this panel before folding it up.) Stitch 1/2" seam along both sides. Zig zag seams. Turn right side out.

E.

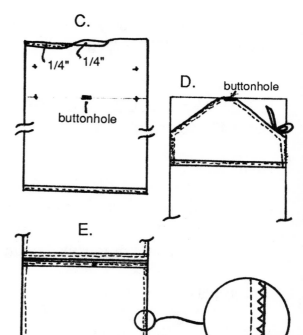

F. Insert clothes hanger through buttonhole.

OPTION:

Use scrap material to applique a design of your choice on the front of the bag before assembling.

HOODED TOWEL WITH WASHCLOTH

-1 yard 60" wide stretch terrycloth
  makes two towels and 4 washcloths
-6 yards of 1/2" or 1" wide double fold bias
  or fabric tape is enough for 1 towel and 2
  washcloths. OR 12 yards will make both
  towels and all four washcloths.

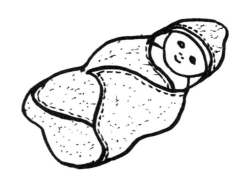

Layout and Cut

A. Make sure cut edges are straight ! !
Measure 10" and 20" from fold on cut edge,
mark. Measure 7" from cut edge on fold and
on selvage, mark. Measure 10" and 20" from
7" mark on fold toward selvage, mark.

B. Cut from 7" mark on selvage to 7" mark
on fold through both layers. From this 7"
strip, cut at fold, at 10" marks, and at 20"
marks. Cut along fold on remaining fabric.

C. Take one of the 7"x10" pieces, fold it in
half widthwise. On one side mark fold.
Draw lines from mark to opposite corners to
form a triangle for the hood. Cut on lines.

A. B.

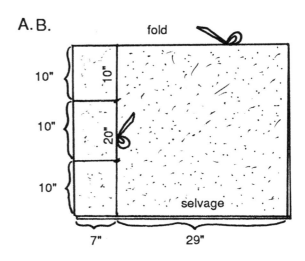

C.

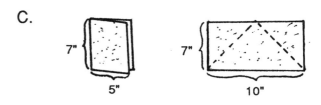

Sewing Directions -
Hood

D. Pin tape to long edge of hood triangle,
stitch. Stitch close to inside edge.

D.

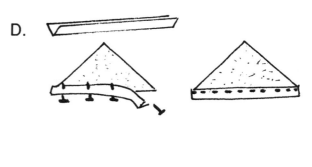

Towel

E. Pin wrong side of hood triangle to one
corner of the terrycloth on right side of
fabric.

E.

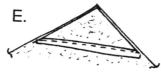

HOODED TOWEL WITH WASHCLOTH
Continued

Edges

F. Pin tape to edges of towel tucking under excess tape at corners. Fold under 1/2" of tape at last corner for a finished edge. Stitch close to inside edge of tape.

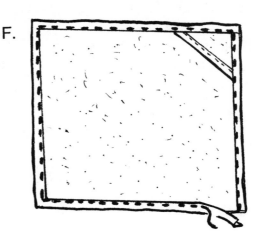

G. Repeat steps C-F for second towel.

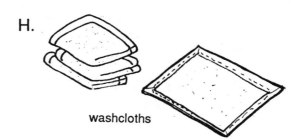

H. Finish four 10"x7" washcloths with bias tape in the same manner as you made the towel.

washcloths

Grow-With-Me Idea: Toddler Poncho

Use this towel as an after bath poncho for a toddler by cutting a hole in the center of the towel.

Fold the towel in half lengthwise and then in half widthwise again. Measure 2" from fold in both directions. Cut curved line between 2" marks. Finish opening with bias tape.

It is great to throw on them before they go charging out the bathroom door.

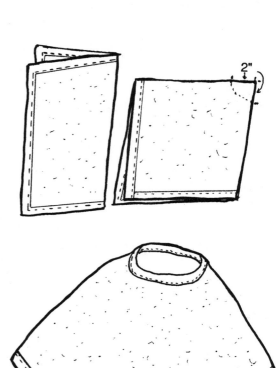

HOODED TOWEL APRON

<u>Make the towel as in the previous pattern then turn it into an apron with the following materials.</u>

-one ribbon 3 feet long
-one ribbon 5 feet long

Marking

A. Lay towel flat on table. From corner next to hood, measure 7" and 19" from corner in both directions. Mark the points.

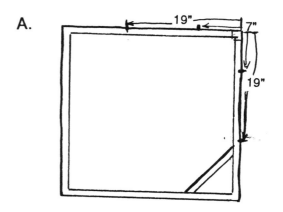

A.

Sewing Directions

B. Lay 3 ft. ribbon across towel between 7" marks. Pin it in place at each edge and in the middle of the towel.

C. Lay 5 ft. ribbon across towel between 19" marks. Pin it in place at each edge and in the middle of the towel.

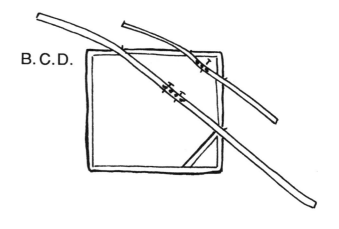

B. C. D.

D. Machine stitch ribbon in place at edges and the middle where you had it pinned.

E. To finish ends of ribbon use frey check or turn under 1/4" and 1/4" again. Stitch next to inside edge.

To Wear

Now you can tie the 3 ft. ribbon around your neck and the 5 ft. ribbon around your waist at bath time and make it easier when you get the baby out of the bath.

This is a SUPER shower gift.

NOTE: Thanks to Mrs. Lucy Rae Franklin for the idea for this pattern.

PARENT'S BATH APRON

-1 towel approximately 24"x27"
-2 yards 1/2" wide double fold bias tape

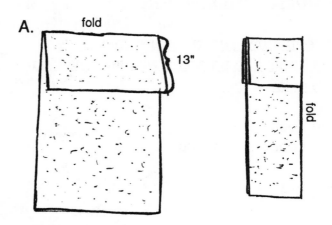

Layout and Cut

A. Position towel so if there is a label, it is face down at the top of the towel. Fold top down 13", then fold in half lengthwise. You will have four layers of towel.

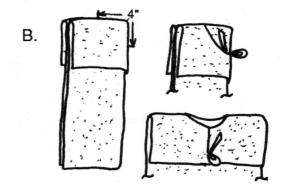

B. On top fold, measure 4" from side fold, mark. On side fold, measure down 4" from top fold, mark. Draw curved line between 4" marks. Cut along this line and along back fold between neck and bottom edge.

C. Make a mark at bottom of folded panel on outside edges (see diagram).

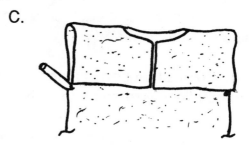

Sewing Directions - Neck

D. Zig zag both cut edges in the back. Turn under 1/2" on both sides of back panel. Zig zag through all layers on top of previous zig zag.

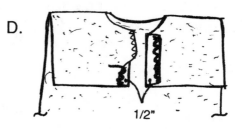

E. Take bias tape, turn under 1/2" at one end. Pin tape around neck. Cut tape 1/2" longer, turn it under to finish other end of tape. Stitch close to inside edge.

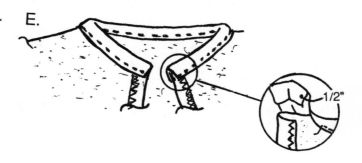

OR

F. Use fabric tape to finish back edges and neck. Turn under 1/2" at one end. Pin tape on cut back edge from bottom finished edge of towel, around neck and down other back edge. Cut tape 1/2" longer, turn it under to finish other end. Stitch close to inside edge of tape.

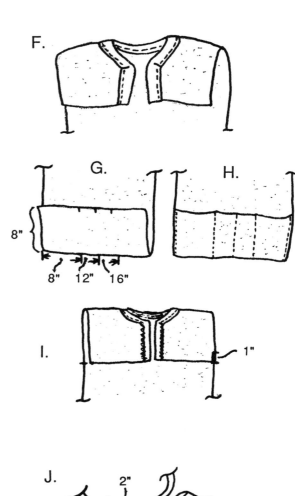

Pockets

G. Fold bottom of towel up 8". Measure in 8", 12", and 16" from left top edge of pocket, mark each point. Measure 8", 12", and 16" from bottom left edge of pocket, mark each point.

H. Stitch side edges from top of pocket to bottom through all layers. Stitch straight line between 8",12", and 16" marks. **OR** make the pockets any width you want, so they will be convenient for what you want to carry in them.

Underarm

I. Match marks on front edges to back corner marks making arm opening. Stitch from bottom edge up 1" and backstitch.

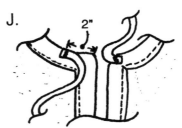

Ties

J. Stitch one 12" tie on the right edge of neck in the back. Stitch the other 2" from back opening at the neck on left side.

BASIC BIBS

-one washcloth per bib
-18" ribbon or fabric tape

Marking

A. Fold washcloth in half. On fold, measure down 2" from top edge. Measure over 2" on top from fold.

Cut

B. Cut curved line from 2" mark on fold to 2" mark on top edge.

Sewing Directions

C. Take 18" of ribbon or fabric tape. Fold tape in half lengthwise. Fold tape over neck edge, pin in place.

D. Turn under 1/4" on each end of tape to the inside to finish ends.

E. Stitch close to open edge of tape.

NOTE: If bibs are too wide, fold under 1 1/2" on each side edge to wrong side. Stitch close to inside edge.

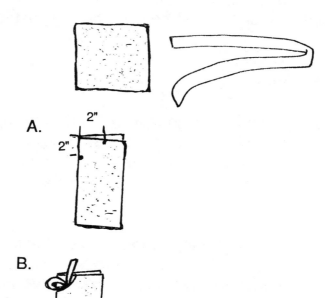

A.

B.

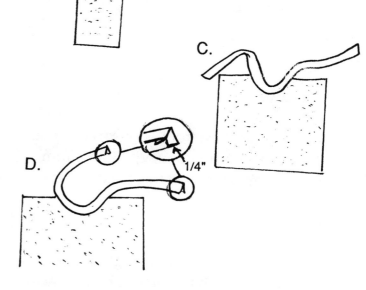

C.

D.

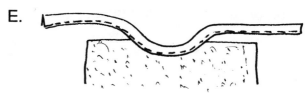

E.

FULL BACK BIB

-two washcloths
-36" of 1/2" fabric tape

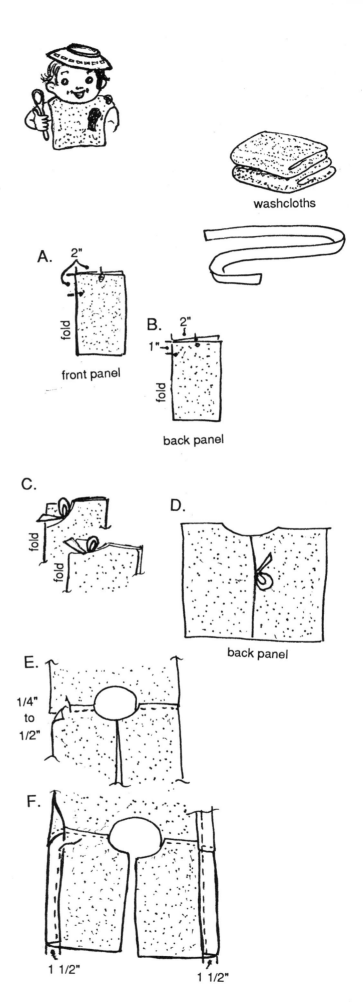

washcloths

Marking

A. Using two washcloths, fold both in half. On one, measure in 2" from fold on top edge, mark. Measure down 2" from top edge on fold, mark. This is the front panel.

A.

front panel

B. On other washcloth, measure in 2" from fold on top edge, mark. Measure down 1" from top edge on fold, mark. This is the back panel.

B.

back panel

Cut

C. Cut curved line from 2" marks on top edges to 1" and 2" marks on fold.

C.

D. Cut back fold of back panel.

D.

back panel

Sewing Directions

E. Overlap top shoulder fabric of the two washcloths by approximately 1/4". Stitch through both layers.

E.

1/4"
to
1/2"

F. Lay cloths flat, face down. Turn under 1 1/2" on each side from bottom back to bottom front. Stitch close to inside edge.

F.

1 1/2"   1 1/2"

FULL BACK BIB Continued

G. Finish raw edges in back and around neck with fabric or bias tape. Take fabric tape, turn under 1/4" on end. Place finished end of tape on raw bottom edge at back opening. Stitch 1/8" from inside edge of tape. Leave 1/2" of tape to turn under and finish end.

H. To close back, place two bottom sections of velcro or snaps on left side of cloth, one on the neck edge, the other 2" to the left. Place one top section on the under side of the right panel.

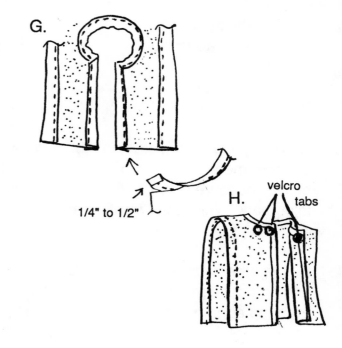

G.

1/4" to 1/2"

H.

velcro tabs

Variation 1:
All bibs can have pockets on front to keep food from flowing down into the lap. Fold bottom edge up 2" and stitch at sides and across bottom.

1.

2"

Variation 2:
If bibs are too wide, fold under 1 1/2" on each side edge to wrong side. Stitch 1/8" from open inside edge.

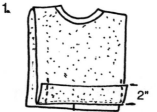

2.

1/8"

1 1/2"

Variation 3:
Instead of a plain edge, put rick rack around the edges or a fabric ruffle, lace or fabric tape.

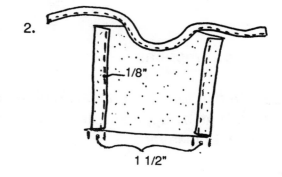

3.

Variation 4:
Applique a design or name on the front of bib.

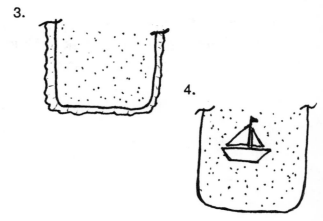

4.

LONG ARM BIBS

-1 hand towel
-2 yards of 1/2" wide double fold bias tape

Layout and Cut

A. Fold top long edge of towel down 5" so wrong sides are together.

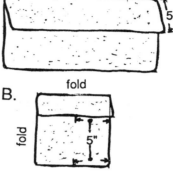

B. Fold in half widthwise with right sides together. Measure 5" from fold on bottom edge and 5" from fold along folded down edge. Mark both points.

Neck

C. On top fold measure 2 1/2" from side fold, mark. Measure 2" down side fold from top fold, mark.

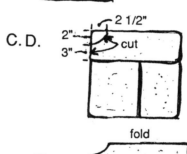

D. Cut curved line from 2 1/2" mark to 2" mark. Cut along remaining 3" back fold.

E. Cut between 5" marks and along edges of towel to side edges.

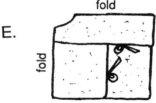

Sewing Directions -
Neck, Side and Back Edges

F. Pin double fold bias tape around neck, side edges and back. Stitch close to inside edge.

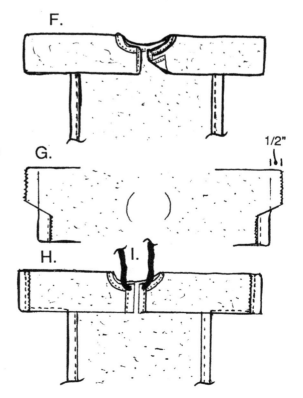

Sleeves

G. Zig zag end of sleeve then turn under 1/2" to wrong side. Stitch close to inside edge.

H. Fold sleeve flap over so wrong sides are together, stitch 1/2" seam along underarm. Zig zag edge. Repeat this step for other sleeve.

I. Stitch a 12" tie at the top on each side of back neck opening.

OVER THE SHOULDER BIB

-one washcloth
-12" of 1/2" wide bias tape
-2 snaps or 2 velcro tab closures

Marking

A. Fold top of washcloth down 3" then fold in half.

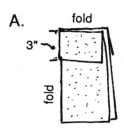
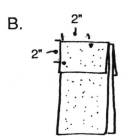

B. On top fold, measure in 2" from back fold, mark. Measure down 2" on back fold, mark.

Cut

C. Cut a curved line from mark on top fold to mark on back fold.

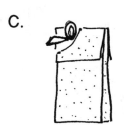
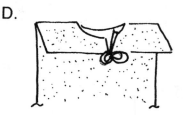

D. On back fold, cut from 2" mark to finished edge of cloth.

Sewing Directions

E. Zig zag cut back edges. Turn under 1/4", zig zag again on top of first zig zag stitching.

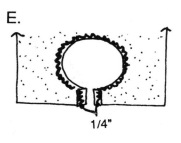

F. Fold under 1/2" on one end of tape. Pin to back edges, around neck and to other back edge. Turn under 1/2" at other end of tape. Topstitch close to inside edge of tape.

Back Closure

G. Use velcro or snaps to close back. Place two bottom tabs on left side of cloth, one on center, the other 2" to the left. Place one top tab on underside of right side of cloth on back edge.

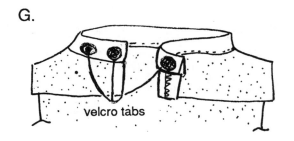

CATCH-ALL

-1 1/2 yards of 45" fabric
-22"x36" piece of super loft quilt
  batting
-1 yard of 1/4" elastic
-9" of bias tape or fabric tape in
  matching color
-22"x36" piece of interfacing

OPTION: Use 1 yard fabric and the center portion of a pre-printed square. Use the top and bottom of the square to make the pockets. Sew them together to make a 9"x45" pocket panel.

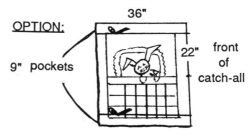

Layout and Cut

A. Cut two 22"x36" pieces for back panels, and one 9"x45" pocket panel. Cut one piece of batting and one piece of interfacing 22"x36".

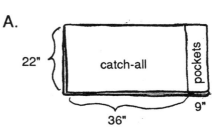

Sewing Directions
Pocket Panel

B. Turn under 1/4" then 1/2" on one 45" side. Stitch 1/8" from inside edge, making a casing.

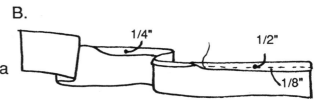

C. Pull 36" of elastic through casing. Stay-stitch elastic at each end.

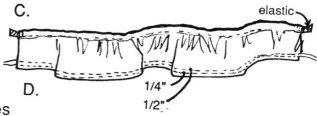

D. Along bottom of pocket, stitch two lines of gathering stitches 1/4" and 1/2" from raw bottom edge.

E. Pull bottom threads to gather evenly to 36" width.

CATCH-ALL Continued

Assembling

F. Place wrong side of gathered pocket strip on right side of one back panel, making sure the gathered edge is along bottom edge of backpanel. Place interfacing on the back side of the back panel.

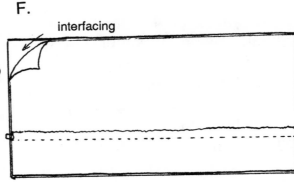

F.

interfacing

G. Pin pocket every 7" along elastic at top and along gathers at the bottom. Stitch from pin on top edge of elastic to pin at the bottom gathers. (OR, you can make these pockets any width you wish to fit the items you plan to put into them.)

G.

stitch lines to form pockets

clip   7"   clip

Finishing Edges

H. Place right sides of catch-all together so pockets are in the middle. Place batting on the bottom next to pocket panel.

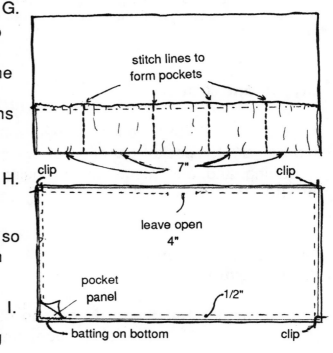

H.

leave open 4"

pocket panel

1/2"

I. Stitch 1/2" seam on 3 1/2 sides leaving 4" opening in center top. Clip corners.

I.

batting on bottom   clip

J. Turn right side out. Stitch 4" opening closed. Stitch 1/8" from outside edge on all four sides.

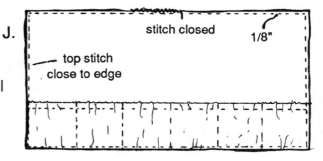

J.

stitch closed   1/8"

top stitch close to edge

Hanging Loops

K. Make fabric tape or use folded bias tape. Cut three 3" pieces of tape. Take one piece at a time and fold so cut edges are together (wrong side of one end to right side of the other end). Making a loop. Zig zag along edge.

K.

zig zag edge

L. Repeat this for the other two hanging loops.

M.

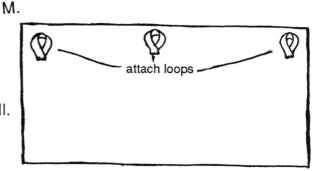

attach loops

M. Place one fabric loop at each edge and one in the middle. Stitch across zig zag edge through loop and all layers of catch-all.

Hanging on Wall

N.

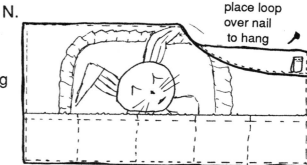

place loop over nail to hang

N. To attach to the wall, hammer nails or picture hooks on the wall above the changing area to correspond with the loops on the back of the catch-all.

To Use

Fill pockets with tubes of ointment, containers of cornstarch, skin lotions, shoes, and TOYS which can entertain the baby during changes.

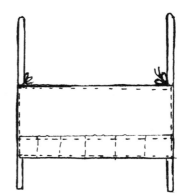

Grow-With-Me Idea:

Use it now over changing table. Use it later by attaching to the end of a bed or on the wall to hold shoes or toys.

CHANGING TABLE PAD

-3/4" thick foam pad
-1 1/2 yards 45" cotton lining

If you have a dresser you want to use as a changing table these directions will help you make a pad and cover to make the surface more comfortable for your baby.

Babies spend so much of their day being dressed, undressed, and changed, that it makes a lot of sense to pad the surface to make the child more comfortable.

Foam Pad

A.

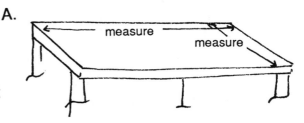

A. Measure the length and width of the dressing table. Most foam you buy will be wider than you need, so cut the foam to fit the top of the table (dresser).

Layout and Cut
Undercover (a thin cover for the pad to give an extra layer of protection)

B. I recommend a plain cotton (an old sheet is fine). Fold your fabric so you have two layers. Mark on your fabric the measurements you had to cut your foam. Add 1 1/2" to the width and 2" to the length. This allows for 1/2" seams and the thickness of the foam.

B.

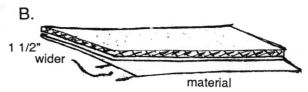

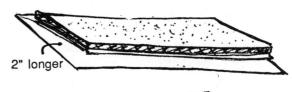

C. Cut the fabric along these lines.

Sewing Directions

D.

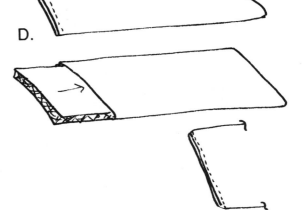

D. Fold fabric in half lengthwise so right sides are together. Stitch seam along side and across one end. Turn right side out, place foam inside. Stitch end closed.

CHANGING TABLE PAD COVER

-1 1/2 yards 45" fabric
-rick rack (optional)

NOTE: This cover is made like a pillow sham so you can take the cover off and wash it without having to wash the whole pad.

Layout and Cut

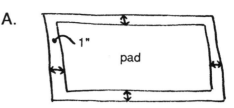

A. You are going to cut one top panel 2" longer and 2" wider then your foam measurement.

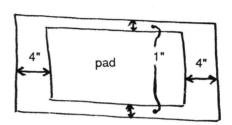

B. For the bottom panel, add 2" to the width and 8" to the length of your pad measurement. Cut it in half widthwise (see diagram).

Sewing Directions

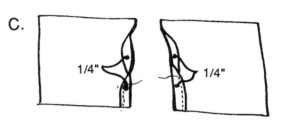

C. Working with the bottom two pieces, fold the edges you just cut to wrong side of fabric 1/4" and 1/4" again, stitch close to the inside edge.

D. Take the top panel and two bottom panels, place them with right sides together so the stitched folds are in the center of the cover and overlap.

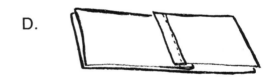

E. Stitch 1/2" seam around the cover. Clip corners. Turn right side out. Place foam pad inside.

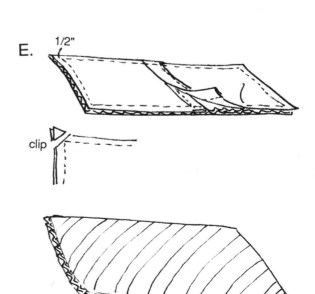

Variation:
For decorative effect, use medium width rick rack, ruffles or lace in the seam. **OR** Applique a design of your choice onto the cover.

Helpful Hint: To help keep this cover clean and help with clean-ups, place a <u>cloth diaper</u> on the surface before laying the baby down. It will absorb and help with clean-ups and you can throw it in the wash.

DIAPER STACKER - CONVENIENT SIZE

-1 1/4 yard 45" fabric
-8"x6"quilt batting
-8" cord, ribbon, fabric or bias tape

NOTE: This stacker can be used with the animal toppers.

Layout and Cut

A. Cut one piece of fabric 45"x32" for the body, one 6"x6" for the bottom and two 8"x6" pieces for topper (or cut pieces for animal topper). Curve top edges of topper. Lay top fabric on top of batting. Cut around topper fabric through batting. (You may want two layers of batting.)

Sewing Directions - Body Panel

B. On 32" sides, turn under 1/4" to wrong side. Topstitch close to inside edge OR finish edges with bias or fabric tape.

C. Stitch two rows of gathering stitches 1/4" and 1/2" from raw edge on both 45" edges.

D. Pull bottom threads. Gather bottom to 24".

Bottom

E. Pin bottom gathered edge around 6"x6" square so that front meets in middle of one side. Stitch 1/2" from edge through all layers of stacker.

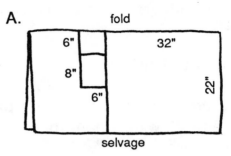

A. fold

6" 32"

8" 22"

6"

selvage

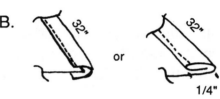

B. 32" or 32"

1/4"

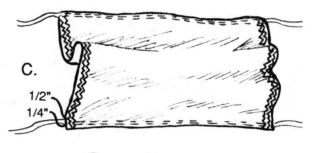

C.

1/2"
1/4"

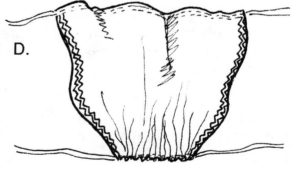

D.

E.

1/2"

DIAPER STACKER TOPPER Continued
Marking

F. Fold one panel in half with wrong sides together. Mark fold on bottom edge and mark 3" up on fold.

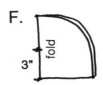

Sewing Directions - Hanging Loop

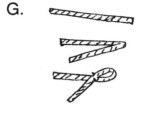

G. Take 8" of cord or fabric/bias tape which has had open edge stitched closed, fold it in half widthwise. Stitch one inch from fold, making a loop.

H. Place loop so stitching is on 3" mark and ends of strip are approximately two inches apart (each 1" from mark on fold).

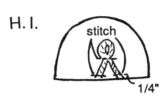

I. Stitch strip in place by stitching on top of stitching, making the loop, and across end of strip in seam allowance - about 1/4" from cut edge.

Assembling Topper

J. Place second fabric piece right sides together with loop panel. Place batting on bottom next to wrong side of front panel. Pin well.

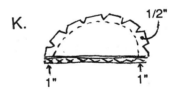

K. Stitch 1/2" seam around topper, backstitch edges. Clip and trim batting and seams as needed. On open edge, clip batting back 1/2".

L. Turn right side out. Press fabric under 1/2" on both front and back.

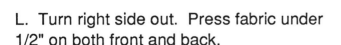

DIAPER STACKER Continued

Attaching Diaper Stacker

M. Gather top of stacker to fit in opening. Pin so front edges meet in middle of the front and all gathers are inside topper.

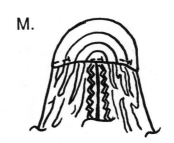

M.

N. Stitch close to edge of topper.

OPTION: You may want to stitch stacker to back panel. Turn topper up. Then stitch thru all layers 1/8" from folded under edge.

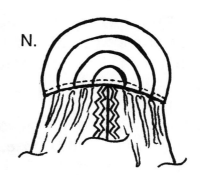

N.

DIAPER STACKER - TWO BOX

-1 1/4 yards fabric, cotton print
-7 feet medium rick rack (optional)

NOTE: This stacker can be used with the animal toppers.

Layout and Cut

A. Cut three 11"x14" rectangles and one 45"x27" rectangle. On 27" fold, measure 2" from cut edge, mark. Draw line from 2" mark on fold to selvage (see diagram).

Sewing Directions - Front Edge

B. Take the 45"x27" panel. Fold selvages 1/2" to wrong side. Stitch close to inside edge.

Bottom

C. Take one of the bottom panels, fold it in half (7"x11") make a mark on both ends of the fold (front and back).

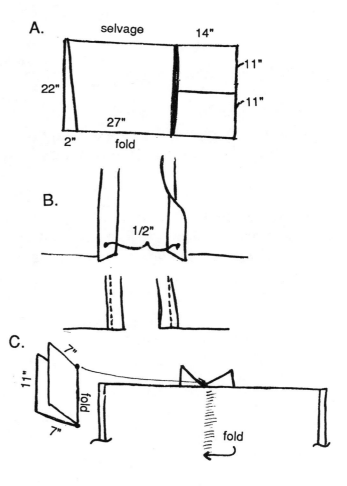

26

DIAPER STACKER - TWO BOX Continued

Assembling

D. Pin stacker panel to bottom panel with right sides together. Match fold of stacker with one mark on bottom panel. Stacker will come to about 1" from each side of front mark. Stitch 1/2" seam. Clip corners.

E. Zig zag raw edge in front opening, continuing around bottom edges of panel.

F. At front opening, turn zig-zagged edge 1/2" to inside (wrong sides together.) Stitch 1/4" from outside edge to finished opening edge. Turn right side out.

G. On top of stacker, machine baste two lines of stitching 1/8" and 1/4" from raw edge. Pull bottom threads to gather top of stacker fabric to 14" width. Fold top so there is 3 1/2" on each side of the front.

Bottom Insert

H. Take other two 11"x14" panels, stitch 1/2" seam on three sides leaving open one of the 14" sides.

I. Turn under 1/4" and 1/4" again on unstitched side. Stitch close to inside edge. Clip corners. Turn right side out.

J. Put 10"x13" cardboard in fabric cover. Place in bottom of diaper stacker so opening is toward the back. Attach diaper stacker topper as stated above Attaching Diaper Stacker step I.

Grow-With-Me Idea:
Use it now as a diaper stacker or later to hold pajamas. Put a box in the bottom to hold toys.

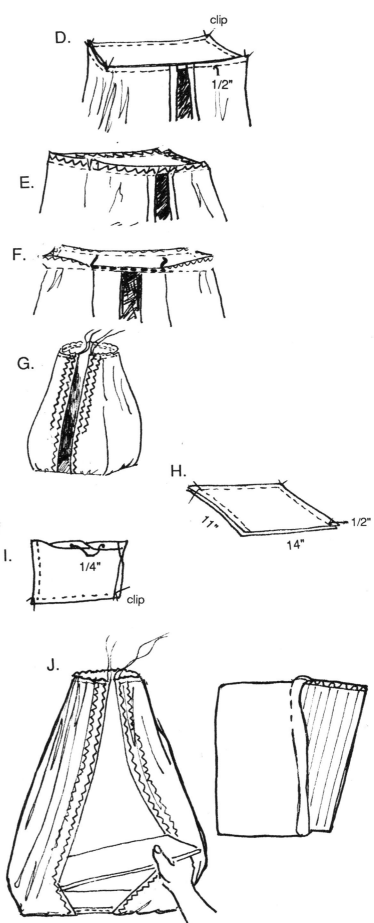

DIAPER TOPPERS-
BEAR, LION, DOG, DUCK, CAT, BUNNY

-1/4 yard fabric
-quilt batting
-scrap fabric for eyes, nose, beak, muzzle etc.
-tear-away interfacing
-glue stitck

These designs are versatile. Use them to coordinate your nursery by making your diaper stacker, applique your crib quilt, pillow, crib headboard, catch-all, and as a topper for a cuddley toy.

Layout and Cut -
Main Color for Design

NOTE: Trace the pattern pieces from the book onto tracing paper. Cut the pieces from the tracing paper saving the patterns in the book.

A.

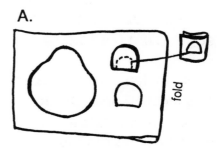

A. Cut two head panels and four ear pieces.

From Coordinate

B. Cut two ear insert pieces from coordinate fabric. **For the Bear** cut a muzzle, **for the Lion**- cut a 2"x70"strip for the mane, **for the Duck** cut one beak.

B.

| bear dog | lion | cat bunny mouse | bear muzzle | duck beak |

Other Fabric

C. All animals require you to cut nose and mouth line from black (except the duck of course). Cut two large eye circles from white and two small circles for eyes from desired color.

2" 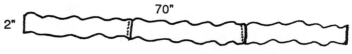 70"

C.

eyes

fold   fold

white   color

From Batting and Interfacing

D. Cut one head panel and two ear pieces from two layers of batting.

D.

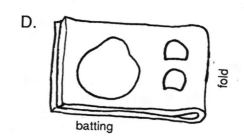

batting

28

DIAPER TOPPERS Continued

Marking

E. On one head, mark dots on right side of fabric where ears, eyes and nose attach. Also mark where to leave open to attach diaper stacker or cuddley. **For Bear** mark where nose attaches on the muzzle piece.

E.

F. On front ear piece, mark where to attach inner ear.

F.
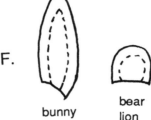

bunny   bear
             lion

Before Sewing

G. Glue color circle for eyes to white circles. Then glue large circle into position on head.

H. Glue nose and mouth onto head as specified. **For Duck** beak attaches at nose mark. **For Bear** glue nose onto muzzle then glue muzzle into positon.

I. Glue ear insert onto the right side of two ear pieces.

G.

H.
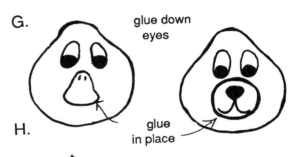

glue down
eyes

glue
in place

I.
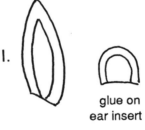

glue on
ear insert

Sewing Directions - Applique

NOTE: If you have never done any applique work before, you might want to practice making an eye on a separate piece of fabric. The color portion of the eye is a little difficult because of having to slowly move your fabric to go around such a small circle

J. Now that you have everything glued into position, place tear-away interfacing on the wrong side of each piece to be appliqued.

J.

interfacing

<u>DIAPER TOPPERS</u> Continued

K. Use a satin zig zag stitch to machine applique the eyes, nose, ear inserts and muzzle for the bear. The closer together your stitches the richer your design will look. Use a medium width to your zig zag stitch.

K.

close together

applique

Ears

L. Place ear pieces right sides together with batting on the bottom. Stitch 1/4" seam around ears. Leave open at the bottom.

M. Trim and clip seams as needed. Turn right side out.

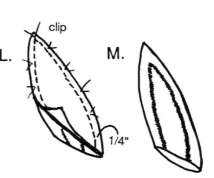

clip

L.   M.

1/4"

Hanging Loop

Note: Skip these steps and go on to assembling directions if making the cuddley.

N. Take a 14" piece of cord, ribbon or bias tape and fold it in half lengthwise. Stitch 1" from fold.

N.

1"

O. Place loop on second head panel so loop is on mark and ends of strip are on marks at bottom of head.

P. Stitch loop in place by stitching across stitching of loop and across end of strip in seam allowance about 1/4" from cut edge.

O.

P.

Assembling Topper

Q. **For Lion,** prepare 70"x2" ruffle for mane by turning under1/4" and 1/4" again on one long edge. Stitch close to turned under edge. On opposite edge, stitch two rows of gathering stitches.

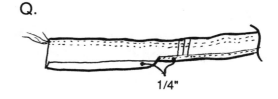

Q.

1/4"

DIAPER TOPPERS Continued

R. Pin ends of strip at opening marks on the bottom of the face. Pin the center of the strip to the top of the face. Pull the bottom threads to fit strip around face. (Ruffle is toward the inside, gathered edge is to the outside around the head.)

R.

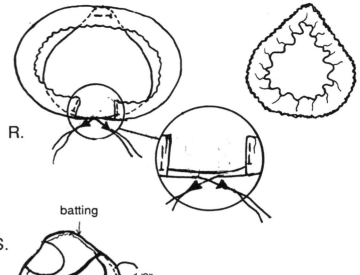

batting

S. **For all toppers,** pin ears on head between marks so ears are toward the inside. Pin head right sides together with batting on the bottom. Make sure hanging loop is toward the top.

S.

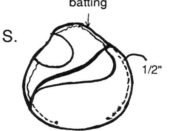

1/2"

T. Stitch 1/2" seam around head. Leave open between dots. Trim seam and clip as needed. Trim away batting between dots at the bottom. Turn right side out.

T.

U. Attach stacker as stated in Diaper Stacker page 26, or soft fabric as stated in Cuddley page 107.

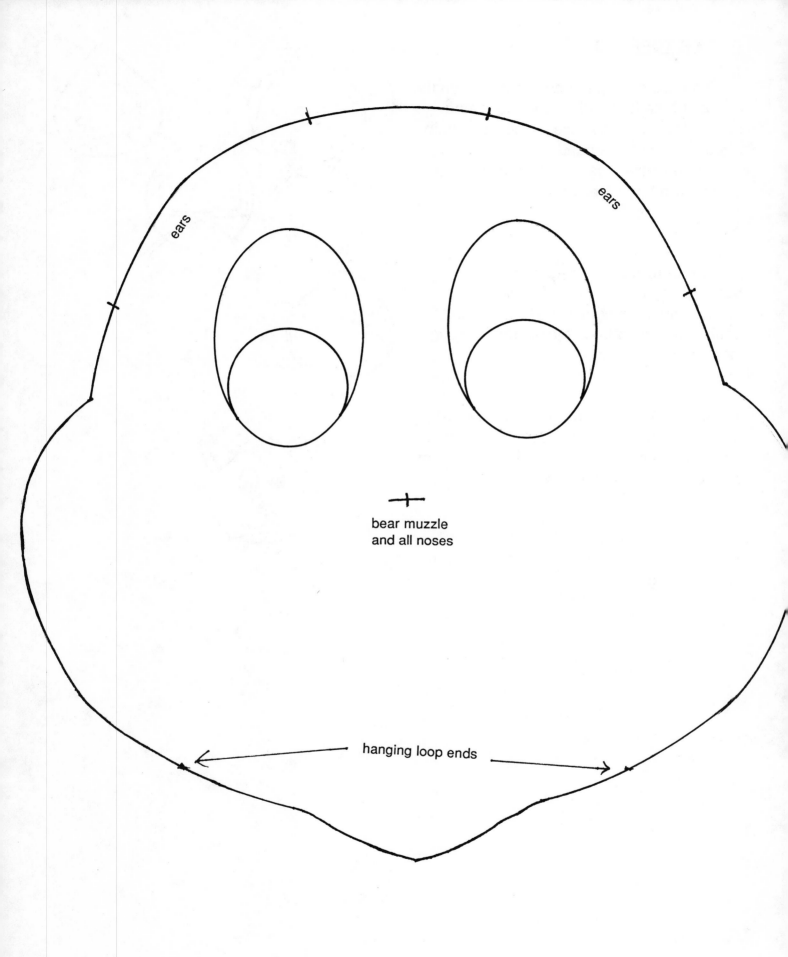

ears

ears

bear muzzle
and all noses

hanging loop ends

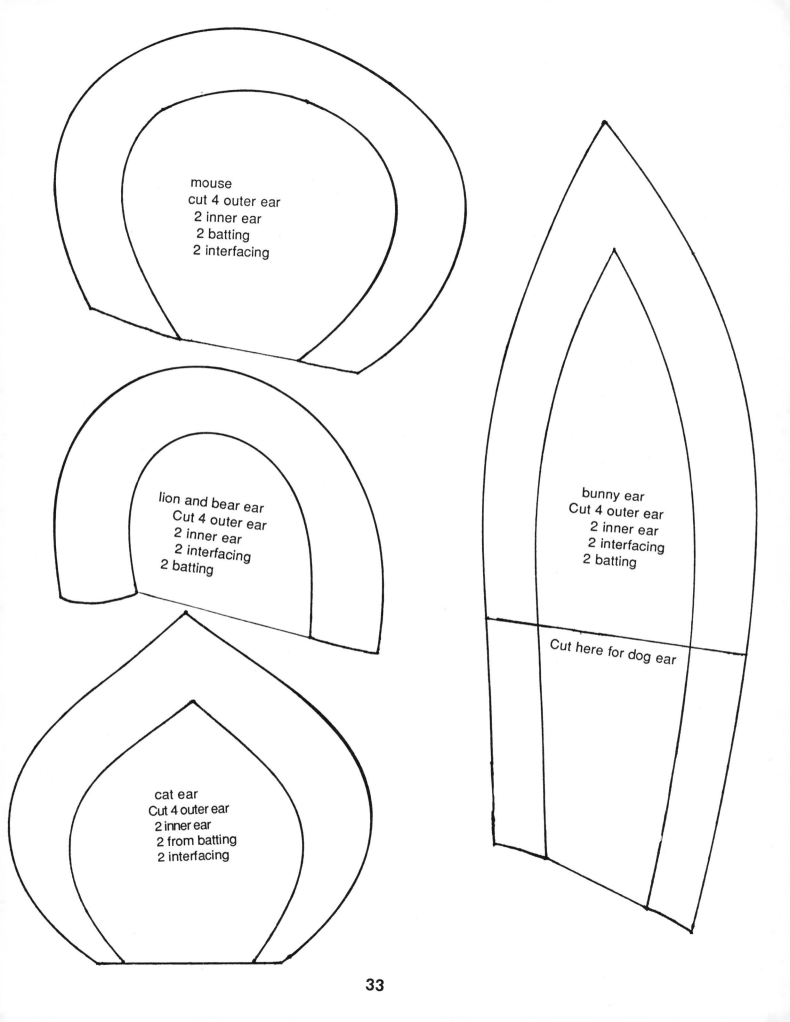

mouse
cut 4 outer ear
2 inner ear
2 batting
2 interfacing

lion and bear ear
Cut 4 outer ear
2 inner ear
2 interfacing
2 batting

cat ear
Cut 4 outer ear
2 inner ear
2 from batting
2 interfacing

bunny ear
Cut 4 outer ear
2 inner ear
2 interfacing
2 batting

Cut here for dog ear

33

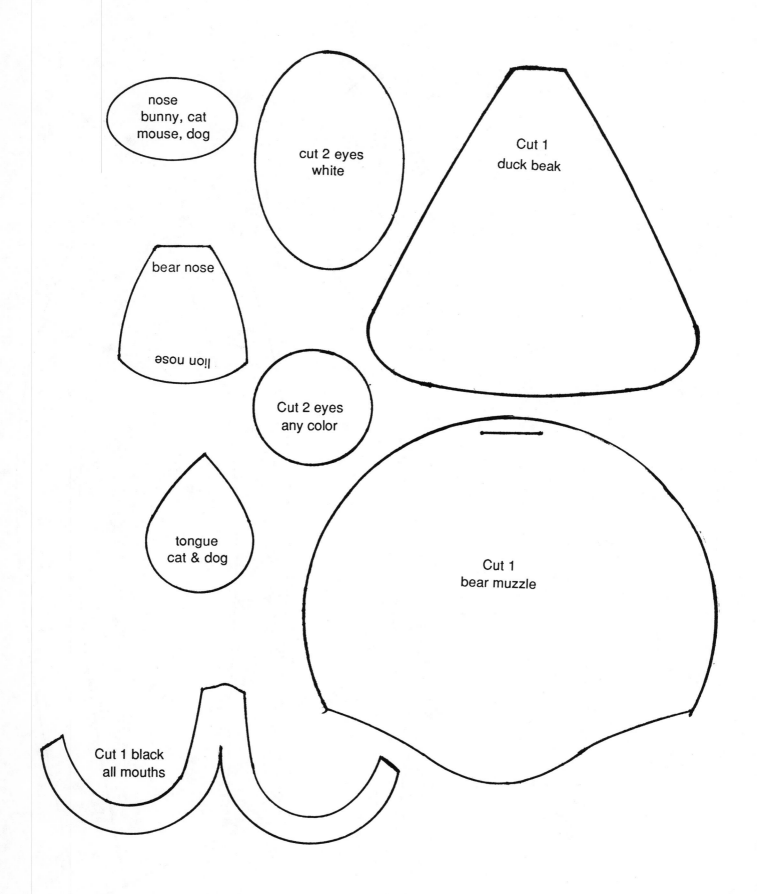

nose
bunny, cat
mouse, dog

cut 2 eyes
white

Cut 1
duck beak

bear nose

lion nose

Cut 2 eyes
any color

tongue
cat & dog

Cut 1
bear muzzle

Cut 1 black
all mouths

34

DIRTY CLOTHES BAG

-1/2 yard 45" fabric
-12" cord, ribbon or double fold bias tape
 or fabric tape

Why use a dirty clothes bag? A Newborn's skin is so sensitive that their clothes are usually washed separately in mild soap. By putting baby's clothes directly in the dirty bag, you don't have to separate them later from the regular wash. "A Time Saver".

Layout and Cut

A. Cut two pieces of fabric 15"x22" for the bag and two 6" pieces of cord or ribbon.

Sewing Directions

B. Place bag pieces right sides together. Stitch one side seam.

C. Turn under 1/2" and 1/2" again on top edge. Stitch close to inside edge.

D. Put right sides together again and stitch remaining side seam and bottom. Turn right side out.

Hanging Loops

E. Take the two 6" cords or ribbon, fold them in half widthwise and attach toward the back side at the side seams.

OPTION: Decorate it with an applique, rick rack in seams, or use ruffles.

GROW WITH ME IDEA:
Use it now for dirty clothes later for a toy bag or a pajama bag. Undo 2" of the top side seam. Backstitch to keep seam from opening more. Pull a cord through the top casing

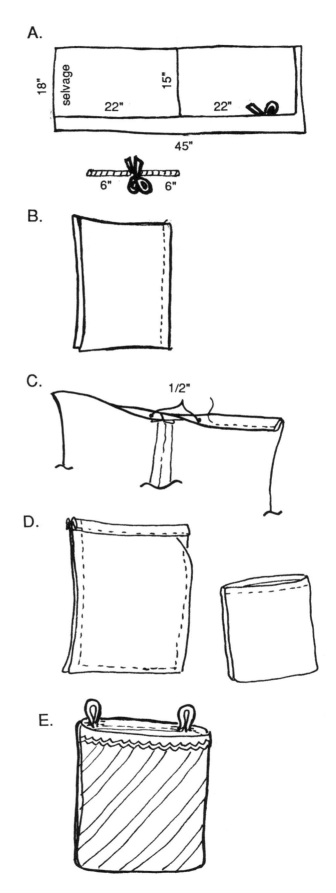

A.

B.

C.

D.

E.

35

BUMPER PADS

-3 3/4 yards 45" fabric
-polyester quilt batting super-loft

NOTE: These bumpers are designed to fit a crib with the inside measurements of 28"x51". If your crib is a different size, adapt the measurements accordingly. You can make them as high as you like, just add 2" in length and width to allow for seam allowance and batting.

DESIGN 1 - For two 13"x26" end pads and two 13"x51" side pads.

Layout and Cut

A. With straight edge and chalk, measure 54" from one end on fold and selvage, mark these points. Measure 15" from selvage toward fold. Mark. Do this at three points along 54" of fabric.

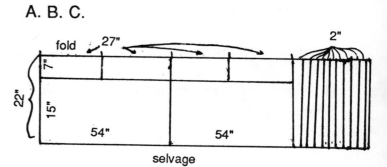

A. B. C.

B. Measure 54 " from first 54" mark on fold and selvage, mark these points. Measure 15" from selvage toward fold along this 54" length. Do this at three points. Connect the marks with a straightedge and chalk as in the diagram. Cut along lines. Cut the two panels that were on the fold in half widthwise so you have four 15"x27" panels.

C. Cut twenty 2"x22" tie downs from remaining fabric.

Batting

D. Cut 3 layers for each panel using the super loft polyester batting. You will need a total of six 15"x52" panels and six 15"x26" panels.

D.

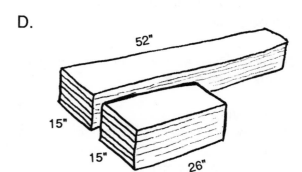

BUMPER PADS Continued

Sewing Directions

E. Make your tie downs by pressing them in half. Fold cut edges in to meet in the middle. Fold on original fold. Stitch close to open edge. Repeat this for all 20 tie-downs.

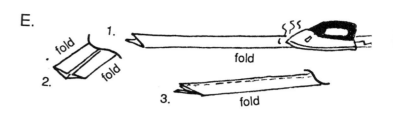

F. Place two side panels right sides together; if using batting place it on the bottom. Pin around all edges. Fold tie downs in half widthwise so you have two 10" ties. Place fold of tie-downs in each corner and in the middle of each side panel so string is toward the inside of the panel. Stitch 1/2" seam around all edges (see Variation 3 if seams are too bulky). Leave open about 12" on bottom edge for turning.

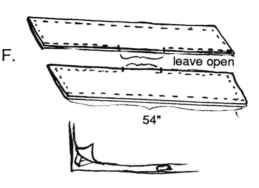

G. Clip corners, turn right side out and stitch opening on the bottom closed.

H. Repeat this for other side panel and end panels. (End panels don't need tie-downs in the middle.)

I. Stitch from top to bottom in the middle of each panel. For side panel, stitch again top to bottom mid-way between ends and middle.

BUMPER PADS - DESIGN TWO - For Six
13"x26" pads

Layout and Cut

A. Mark and cut the fabric the same as in the first design. However, cut the 54" strips in half widthwise so you have six pairs of 15"x27" panels.

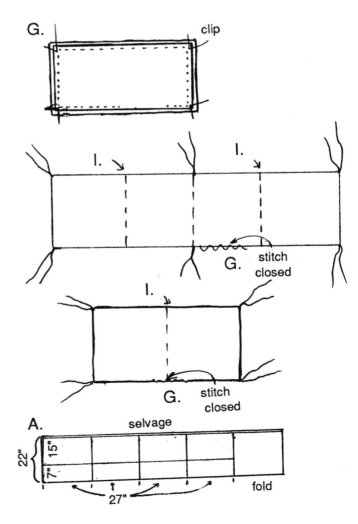

37

BUMPER PADS-DESIGN TWO Continued

B. Cut batting so you have three layers for each 15"x27" panels.

Sewing Directions

C. Assemble each panel as discribed in design one.

D. Stitch row of stitching from top to bottom in the middle of each panel.

Variation 1: For Either Design

Add fabric ruffle, lace, or rick rack in top seam. Or, you can put it on three or all four sides.

Variation 2: For Either Design

Instead of one of the end bumper pads, make the Decorative Headboard (see page 44).

Variation 3: For Either Design

Assemble the bumper pads as above however, stitch the tie downs on last if your machine has difficulty stitching through the layers. This may be easier because you can move the tie away from the seam allowance.

Grow-With-Me Idea:
If you have the bed next to the wall, attach them to the wall for decoration and comfort
or use as throw pillows.

B.

batting

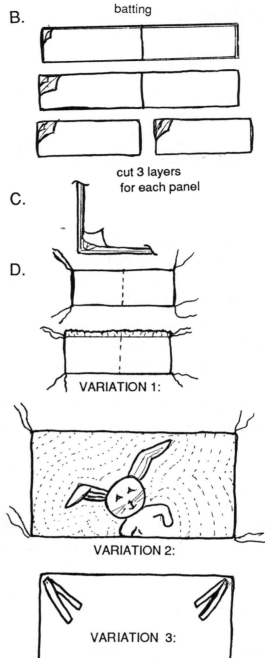

cut 3 layers
for each panel

C.

D.

VARIATION 1:

VARIATION 2:

VARIATION 3:

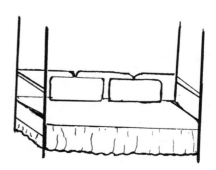

CANOPY

-3 1/2 yards of 45" fabric **OR**
 4 yards for fuller ruffles

Layout and Cut

A. Cut one piece of fabric 31"x58" for top of
canopy. Cut six strips 10"x45" for ruffle
around canopy or eight strips if you want it
fuller.

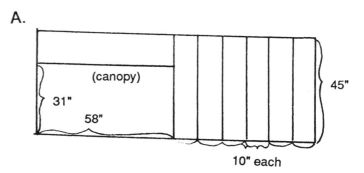

Sewing Directions - Ruffle

B. Take two 10"x45" strips, place them
right sides together. Stitch 1/2" seam on
one 10" side.

C. Open out, place another 10"x45" strip
right sides together with one of the already
joined pieces. Stitch 1/2" seam on the 10"
side. Continue this until all strips are
joined forming one continuous strip.

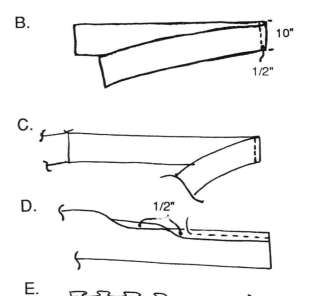

Hem

D. Turn under 1/2" and 1/2" again on one
side (what will be the finished edge of
ruffle). Stitch close to inside edge.

Gathers

E. On unfinished edge, stitch two rows of
gathering stitches 1/4" and 1/2" from raw
edge. Pull bottom threads to gather.

CANOPY Continued

Assembling

F. Place right side of ruffle against right side of canopy top. If you are using six strips, have one seam meet at each corner of canopy and one in the middle of each side (see diagram). Ease ruffles to fit.

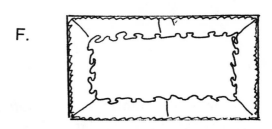

F.

G. If using eight strips, position one strip in the middle of each end and one in the middle of each side, leaving one panel to ease between side and end panels. Stitch 1/2" seam around all edges. Zig zag edges to prevent ravelling.

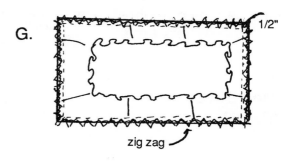

G.   1/2"

zig zag

H. At each corner, measure in 1" from each side. Make 1/2" buttonhole at this mark to allow for canopy to be connected.

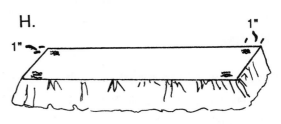

H.   1"

1"

Variation: Double Ruffle

If you would like a double tier canopy you will need to cut the second tier 7" wide. Connect the panels as in B, C, and D. Stitch gathering stitches as in E. Finish canopy as in F through I. Placing short tier right side together with canopy cover with the 10" tier on top of the 7" tier. Place gathering edge to the outside with the ruffle to the inside to stitch seam.

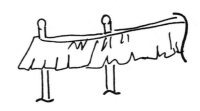

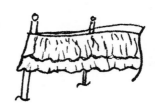

COMFORTER

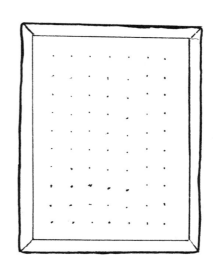

-2 1/2 yards flannel or 1/2 sheet blanket or
  other desired fabric.
-quilt batting-super loft
-embroidery floss **OR** 3 yards of 1/4" ribbon

A baby blanket that has become my favorite is the comforter. It is an ideal weight for an infant. It is easy to make and can be personalized for a great gift.

Here are a few different ways you can make them.

DESIGN 1- Plain Top

Layout and Cut

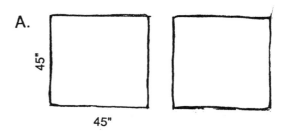

A. Cut two pieces of flannel 45"x45" (These can be of two different colors if you wish or cut a sheet blanket.)

Sewing Directions

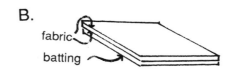

B. Place flannel right sides together with batting on the bottom.

C. Stitch 1/2" seam around three and a half sides leaving 8" open in middle of fourth side. Clip corners.

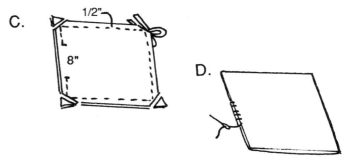

D. Turn right side out. Hand stitch opening closed.

Finishing

E. Use embroidery floss or yarn. Tie knots through all layers every 4".

Variation - Fabric tape finished edge

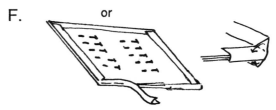

F. Use bias or fabric tape and pin the layers together so batting is between the two layers of flannel.

41

COMFORTER-Variation Continued

G. Pin tape around outside of comforter folding tape at corners. Stitch close to inside edge.

G.

G.

H. Cut ribbon into 4" pieces. Stitch the center of each ribbon through the three layers of fabric every four to six inches. Tie ribbons in bow or knot.

H.

H.

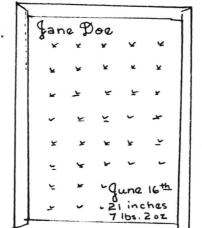

Personalizing

I. Embroider name, birthdate, weight and length of child in a corner. **OR**, use two corners and put two items in each, OR put one item in each corner. Take your pick!!!

Thanks to DeeDee Patz for this special baby gift to my first child. It has been very special and has held up through three children.

I.

COMFORTER DESIGN TWO - Patchwork Top

-Use your remnants or purchase fabric in three different designs (gingham, flower and solid). Use your imagination.

Materials - 28"x40" Comforter
-1/2 yard of three different fabric designs
-1 yard of one of the above for the back
-6 yards 1/4" wide ribbon
-quilt batting-super loft

56"x40" Comforter
-1 yard of three fabrics
-1 5/8 yard of one of above
-12 yards 1/4" wide ribbon
-quilt batting-super loft

NOTE: If using your own remnants you will need the fabric for backing and ribbon. The small comforter is exactly crib size. The larger comforter is twice as large and can be used in the crib or later as a throw on a twin bed.

COMFORTER - DESIGN TWO Continued
Layout and Cut

A. For a 28"x40" comforter, cut 5" squares as follows: 23 squares from two fabrics, 24 squares from one fabric totaling 70 squares.

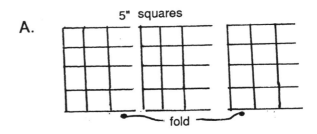

For a 56"x40" comforter, cut 5" squares, 47 squares from two fabrics and 46 squares from one fabric totaling 140 squares.

Sewing Directions- Assembling blocks

B. Place fabric squares right sides together open out. Stitch 1/2" seam on one edge. Place third square right sides together with two stitched squares. Stitch 1/2" seam on one edge. Continue until you have seven strips of ten squares or 14 strips of ten squares. Press seams open.

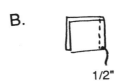

Assembling Strips

C. Place two strips right sides together matching up seams between blocks. Stitch 1/2" seam down one side of strip.

D. Open joined strip, place another strip right sides together with one strip. Stitch down side of strip. Continue until all strips are joined.

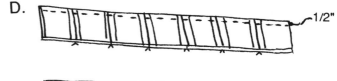

Assembling the Layers

E. Lay assembled top panel on top of quilt batting. Cut batting to fit size of top panel. (You may want more than one layer of batting depending on how thick you want it.)

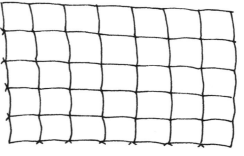

F. Finish the comforter in one of the two methods given in Design 1- plain edge or tape edge. If you choose the plain edge, you can place eyelet, fabric ruffle or rick rack in the seam when stitching.

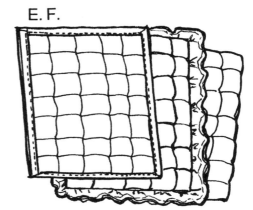

DECORATIVE HEADBOARD

Children spend alot of time in their cribs not only sleeping but playing before and after naps. To add a little bit of color and continuity to the nursery, use a remnant piece of pre-quilted fabric or quilt one yourself and make this decorative headboard for your baby's crib.

Materials

-1 yard bumper pad fabric
-1 brightly printed fabric panel to
  coordinate with bumper pad fabric
-quilt batting

NOTE: If using a scrap piece of pre-quilted fabric, trim it to 27"x22". You will still need 1 yard of your bumper pad fabric.

Layout and Cut

A. Cut one 27"x22" front panel from a pre-printed design fabric panel, one from batting (you may want to cut out more than one layer depending on how lofty you want the headboard) and one from bumper pad fabric. Cut two 2"x20" tie downs.

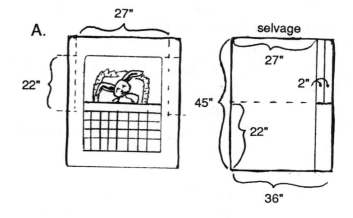

Sewing Directions

B. Place front fabric panel right sides together next to the pre-printed design with batting on the bottom. Stitch 1/2" seam around design leaving 6" open in bottom seam. Clip corners and turn right side out. Stitch the opening closed.

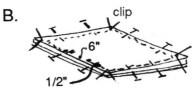
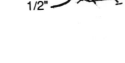

Quilting

C. Pin the layers together, then stitch around the design through all layers. This can be done either by machine or by hand.

quilt around

44

Tie straps

D. Take two 20" tie straps. Fold long sides so they meet in the middle of the strap. Fold in half, stitch close to outside edges.

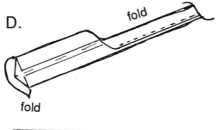

E. Fold in half so you have two 10" ties. Place fold at top corner. Stitch across the fold through all layers. Repeat this for tie in the other top corner.

F. Finish ends with fray check or zig zag.

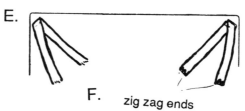

Grow-With-Me Idea:
Machine outline pre-printed fabric panel into decorative headboard later to be used as a pillow sham.

Materials

-1 yard bumper pad fabric
-1 brightly printed fabric panel to
  coordinate with bumper pad fabric
-27"x22" muslin or sheeting
-quilt batting
-1" thick pad 25"x20"
*If using a scrap piece of pre-quilted fabric, trim it to 27"x22". You will still need 1 yard of your bumper pad fabric.

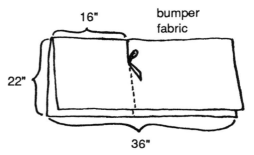

Layout and Cut

A. Cut two 16"x22" back panels from bumper pad fabric. Cut one 27"x22" front panel from a printed design fabric panel, one from batting and one from muslin or other sheeting (this is going to be on the inside and not seen.) Cut two 2"x20" tie downs.

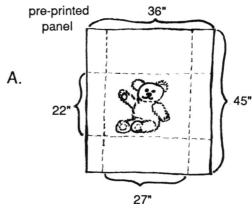

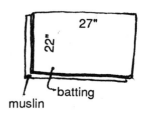

DECORATIVE HEADBOARD - GROW-WITH-ME Continued

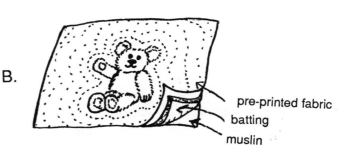

B.

pre-printed fabric
batting
muslin

Sewing Directions - Front

B. Place pre-printed front panel wrong sides together with muslin with batting in the middle. Pin well then machine stitch around the design through all layers. This accents the design.

Back Panels

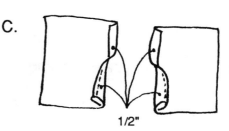

C.

1/2"

C. Turn under 1/2" and 1/2" again on one 22" edge of both back panels.

D. Place front panel right sides together with the two bottom panels, so the finished edges are in the center and overlap.

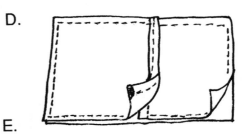

D.

E.

E. Stitch 1/2" seam around the cover. Clip corners. Zig zag edge. Turn right side out.

Ties

F. Make fabric ties by folding each tie in half lengthwise. Fold each edge in to meet on pressed fold. Fold on original fold and stitch close to edge. Zig zag ends.

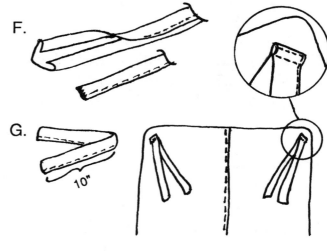

F.

G.

10"

G. Fold in half so you have two 10" tie downs. Place fold at top corner. Stitch across the fold through all layers. Repeat this for tie in the other top corner.

H. To make the headboard thicker while used in the crib insert a 1" thick foam pad or several layers of batting.

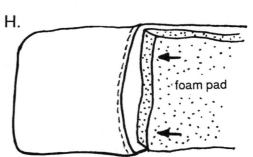

H.

foam pad

46

DUST RUFFLE
DESIGN 1 - Quick and Easy

The easiest way I have found to make a dust ruffle for a baby crib is to attach the ruffle to the top hook of the crib where the springs attach (where you raise and lower the mattress). This avoids hassel with hemming as you lower the mattress. It also helps if you need a place to hide any boxes.

-1 1/2 yards 45" fabric
-50" seam binding
-2" of 1/4" elastic

A.

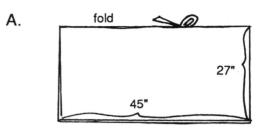

Layout and Cut

A. Cut two lengths of fabric 27"x45"

B.

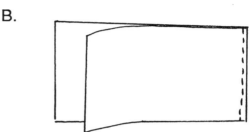

Sewing Directions

B. Place fabric right sides together and stitch side seam (27" seam).

C.

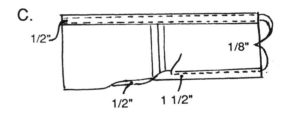

C. Turn under 1/2" then 1 1/2" to wrong side on both top and bottom. Stitch close to inside edge. On top seam, stitch 1/2" from top edge forming a casing.

Hanging Loop Strip

D.

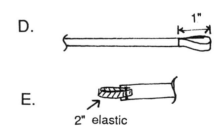

D. Take 50" of seam binding and turn under 1" at one end. Stitch close to cut end through both layers of elastic to make a loop.

E.

2" elastic

E. At other end of binding, fold 2" of elastic in half. Insert binding between the two ends of elastic. Stitch close to edge of elastic through both layers of elastic and the binding.

F.

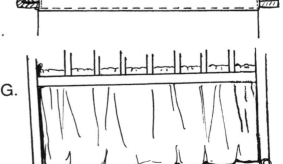

F. Insert binding into top fabric casing.

G. Attach loops over hooks at each end of the crib. Adjust gathers evenly across length of bed.

G.

DUST RUFFLE DESIGN 2 - TWO SIDED

For a ruffle on both sides , you need:
- 3 1/2 yards cotton fabric
OR 4 1/2 yards for a fuller ruffle

NOTE: If you have and old sheet or 1 1/2 yard of white material you can cut the under bed panel from it and only need 2 yards for the ruffle or 3 yards for a fuller ruffle. No one will see the panel under the mattress.

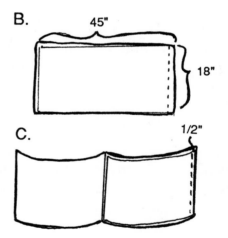

Layout and Cut

A. Cut four 18"x45" panels for side ruffles and one 28"x52" panel for under mattress panel. Cut six 18"x45" side ruffles for fuller ruffle. Mark center of each side of the under mattress panel.

Sewing Directions - Side Panels

B. Connect side panels, by placing two panels right sides together. Stitch 1/2" seam along 18" side.

C. Repeat this step for ruffle on other side. For fuller ruffle, open out panels and place third panel right sides together with one of the panels. Stitch 1/2" seam. Mark top middle of side panel.

Ruffle - Outside Edges

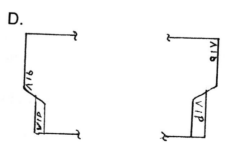

D. If your fabric has no printing in the selvage, there is no need to finish the edge. If there is printing in the selvage of your fabric, turn it under until it is not seen on the front. Stitch close to inside edge.

DUST RUFFLE - TWO SIDED Continued
Hemming

E. Turn under 1/4" and 1/4" again on the bottom of the ruffle panels. Stitch close to inside edge.

Gathering Ruffle

F. Along top edge, stitch two rows of stitches 1/4" and 1/2" from edge.

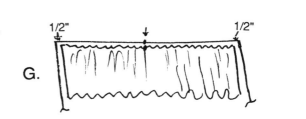

G. Place ruffle right sides together with under-mattress panel so ruffle is along 52" length. Match center seam of ruffle with center mark of under mattress panel. Pin. Leave 1/2" on each end of mattress panel. We will finish it later. Pull bottom threads of ruffle to gather. Adjust fullness while pinning in place.

H. Stitch 1/2" seam then zig zag edge.

I. Repeat steps F-H for ruffle on other side.

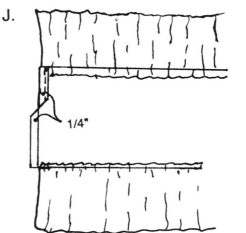

Ends of Undermattress Panel

J. Turn under 1/4" and 1/4" again on unfinished ends of undermattress panel. Stitch close to inside edge.

DUST RUFFLE DESIGN 3 - FOUR SIDED

For ruffle on all four sides you need:
- 4 1/2 yards
OR 5 1/2 yards for a fuller ruffle

NOTE: If you have an old sheet or 1 3/4 yard of white material you can cut the under bed panel from it and only need 3 yards for the ruffle or 4 yards for a fuller ruffle.

DUST RUFFLE - FOUR SIDED Continued

Layout and Cut

A. Cut 6 lengths of fabric 18"x45" (1 for each end and 2 for each side). Cut one 28"x52" panel for under the mattress. Mark center of each end of the under-mattress panel. For a fuller ruffle cut 8 side panels (1 for each end and 3 for each side).

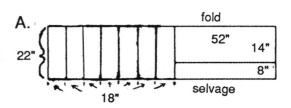

Sewing Directions - Side Ruffles

B. Make ruffle as stated above in steps B-H page 48 and 49.

End Ruffles

C. Take one ruffle panel, finish selvage edge if needed. Hem ruffle by turning under 1/4" and 1/4" again. Stitch close to inside edge. Mark center top of ruffle. Stitch 2 rows of gathering stitches 1/4" and 1/2" from top edge.

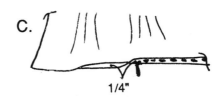

D. Repeat step C for last ruffle panel.

E. Match center mark of undermattress pad with center of ruffle panel. Gather to fit. Pin so there is 1/2" at each end of the ruffle. Stitch 1/2" seam. Zig zag seam edges plus the remaining fabric at the corners between the panels.

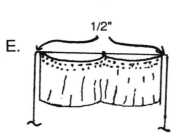

Grow-With-Me Idea:

Later if you would like to make a twin dust ruffle using your crib dust ruffle, purchase an extra yard of ruffle fabric and 1 1/2 yards for the undermattress panel.

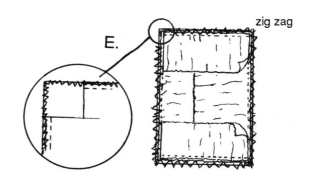

HOOP HEADBOARD

-3 1/8 yard of 45" fabric
-24" of 1/4" or 1/2" ribbon or cord
-1/2 of a hula hoop
-3 nails

Layout and Cut

A. Cut fabric so you have two 45"x1 1/2 yard pieces. The extra 1/8 yard is to make sure you have enough in case your cut edges were not straight when you purchased your material.

A.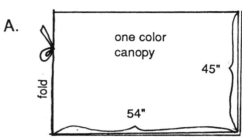

Sewing Directions - Assembling

B. Place 45"x 1 1/2 yard pieces right sides together. Stitch 1/2" seam along 1 1/2 yard length.

B.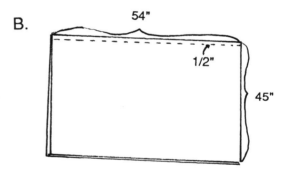

Finishing Top and Bottom

C. On top and bottom turn under 1/2" and 1/2" again. Stitch close to turned under edge. Turn under 1/2" along side edges. If your outside selvage edges do not have printing in them, it is not necessary to finish them.

C.

Hoop Casing

D. Measure and mark on wrong side of fabric 8" up from bottom edge at sides, center seam and folds.

E. Fold fabric at these marks so wrong sides are together. Stitch on right side of fabric 1 1/2" from folded edge from one side to the other. This is making the casing to insert the hoop.

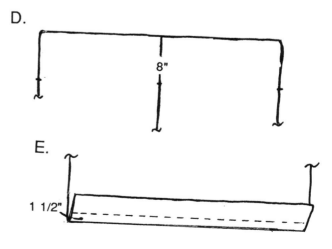

HOOP HEADBOARD Continued

Top Gathering Casing

F. Measure down 3 1/2" from top at side edges, seam and fold. Mark each point.

G. Make two 1/2" buttonholes 1" from center seam at the 3 1/2" mark.

H. Fold fabric at 3 1/2" marks so wrong sides are together. Stitch 1/2" from fold from one side to the other.

Hanging Cord

I. Mark the midpoint of 24"x1/4" of cord or ribbon. If cord or ribbon might ravel treat the ends with fray check.

J. Using safety pin fastened to one end of the cord, pull one end through one side of the casing and through the buttonhole in the center front.

K. Take the other end of the cord with safety pin attached and pull it through the other side of the casing and through the other buttonhole. The midpoint mark of the cord should be in the back to hang on a nail.

L. Pull fabric tightly and tie into a bow.

Hanging

M. Cut hula hoop in half. Insert hoop into casing of material.

N. Put the headboard on the wall in the position you like. Mark on the wall where the midpoint of the gathering cord/ribbon is and where the hoop hits the wall on each side.

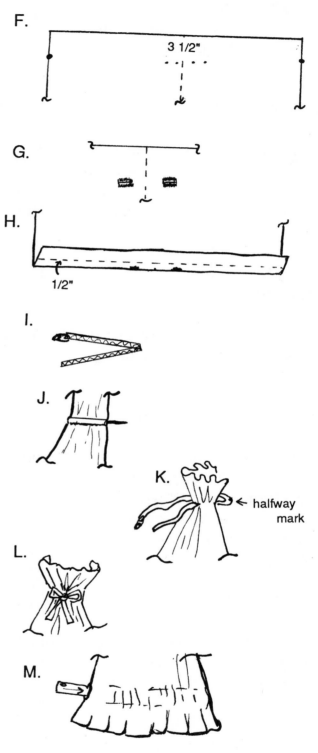

HOOP HEADBOARD Continued

O. Put a nail in the wall at each point. Put the cord over the top nail. Place open ends of the hula hoop over nails so hoop is at a 90' angle to the wall.

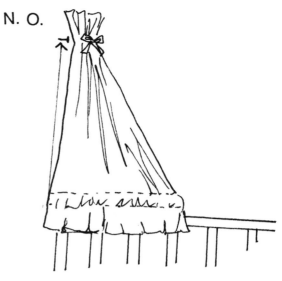

HOOP HEADBOARD - TWO COLORS

-1 5/8 yard of two different fabrics
-1/2 hula hoop
-24" of 1/4" or 1/2" cord or ribbon
-3 nails

Layout and Cut

A. Cut one of the colors along the fold so you have two 22 1/2"x1 1/2 yard pieces which will be the side panels and one 45"x1 1/2 yard piece which will be the center panel. The extra 1/8 yard is to make sure you have enough in case your cut edges were not straight when you purchased your material.

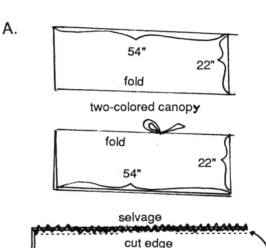

A.

two-colored canopy

Sewing Directions

B. Place side panels right sides together with center panel so cut edges are with selvage. The selvages of the side panels will meet in the middle. Stitch 1/2" seam along length. Zig zag both seams.

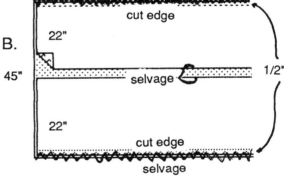

B.

C. Finish the headboard as stated beginning at Step C above.

OPTION: Put an applique in the center panel. (Or on the seam in the middle of the headboard.)

Grow-With-Me Idea:
Use the hoop over the top of the bed or over the middle of the bed if it is against the wall.

OPTION:

QUILTS

There are so many different ways to make quilts it is difficult to know where to begin. I will try to give you several ideas of different quilts you can make.

APPLIQUE DESIGN

-applique a design onto a 36"x45" piece of fabric
-one 36"x45" piece of fabric
-non-woven tear-away interfacing
-quilt batting
-5 yards of 1" double fold bias tape
   OR make fabric tape
-glue stick

Layout and Cut

A. Cut applique design from desired fabric. Arrange and glue onto one 36"x45" piece of fabric.

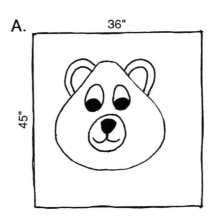

A. 36" 45"

Sewing Directions - Applique

B. Place interfacing to the wrong side of the fabric behind applique design. Stitch around the design to keep it in place. Then use a close together medium wide satin zig zag stitch to finish around the design. The closer the stitches are together the richer the finished look.

B. tear-away close together too far apart

Assembling

C. Place embroidered fabric on top of quilt batting; cut around edge of fabric. (You may want two or even three layers of batting depending on how thick you want your quilt to be.) Place wrong side of quilt backing to the batting.

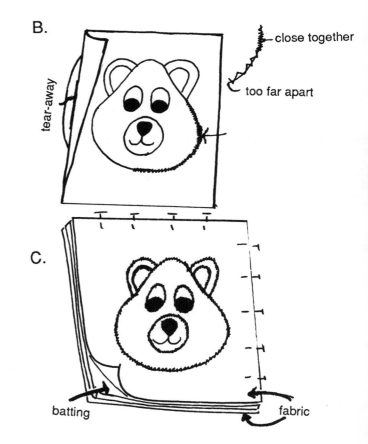

C. batting fabric

QUILTS - APPLIQUE DESIGN Continued

Quilting

D. Pin the three layers together well. Stitch around your design. You may want to stitch about 3" to the outside of your design to accent your applique and to keep the layers of your quilt together.

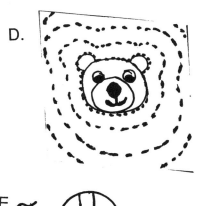

D.

Finishing Edge

E. Pin tape to edge of the quilt. To miter the corners make a tuck in the tape. Fold the tucks over the top of the next side.

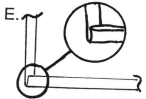

E.

F. At the last corner, cut the tape 1/2" longer and turn it under so the end of the tape will have a finished edge.

G. Stitch tape to quilt close to the inside edge.

G.

F.

1/2"

PATCHWORK DESIGN

-stitch your favorite design to 36"x45"
   OR use a pre-printed fabric square
-one 36"x45" piece of fabric
-quilt batting
-5 yards of 1" double fold bias tape
     OR make fabric tape

Layout and Cut

A. Layout, cut and assemble the quilt design of your choice into a 36"x45" finished size.

Sewing Directions

B. Assemble your quilt as described in Steps C-G above.

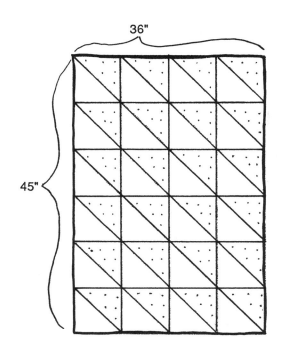

36"

45"

QUILTS PRE-QUILTED FABRIC

-1 square of pre-quilted 35"x42" (cotton on
 both sides)
-1"wide double fold bias tape

Idea: Purchase an extra panel plus two yards of each of
two coordinating colors to make twin size quilt top for a
youth room.

Layout and Cut

A. Cut edges of quilt if they are not straight.

Sewing Directions

B. Pin tape around square folding tape at
corners to fit. Stitch close to inside edge.

Variation - Plain Finished Edge

A. Place stitched panel right sides together
with back fabric with batting on the bottom.
Stitch 1/2" seam around three and a half
sides. Leave 8" open in middle of bottom
edge to turn right side out.

B. Clip corners, trim seams and batting.
Turn right side out. Handstitch opening
closed.

C. Pin well,then stitch around designs.

Ruffled Edge

Before stitching seam, place fabric ruffle or
eyelet lace in seam so the ruffle is to the
inside. Complete as stated in Variation
above.

Grow-With-Me Idea:
Don't put that quilt in the closet! Attach fabric loops to the
top of the quilt and hang it on the wall. Don't worry that it
looks a little faded. It will have a country affect.

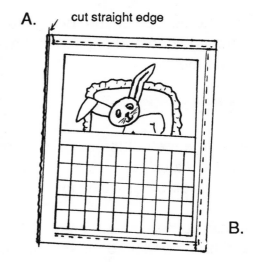

A. cut straight edge

B.

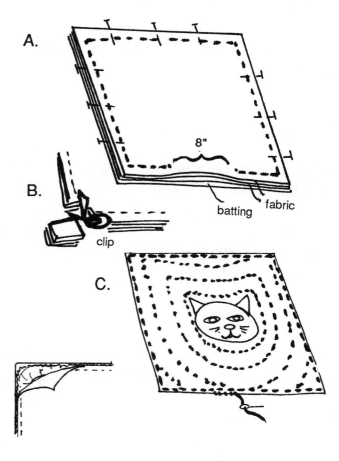

A.

B.

8"

batting   fabric

clip

C.

RECEIVING BLANKETS

-1 1/4 yards flannel OR
-2 1/2 yards for double thickness (see
  Money Saver Tips)

Babies need all kinds of blankets and probably the most versatile is the receiving blanket. Ones you buy in the stores are usually so small that you can only use them for a few months. These receiving blankets you can make large enough to use quite awhile. You can also make them single or double thickness to better suit your purpose.

Single Thickness

A. Use a single thickness of flannel 45"x45". Zig zag raw edges. Press under 1/4" on all sides. Zig zag again on all four sides.

OR

B. Finish edges with bias or fabric tape as in the quilt Design 1 steps B-G.

Double Thickness

C. Use a double thickness of flannel. Two 45"x45" pieces. Place right sides together and stitch a 1/2" seam on three and a half sides leaving 8" open in the middle of the fourth side. Clip corners.

D. Turn right side out. Stitch close to outside edge.

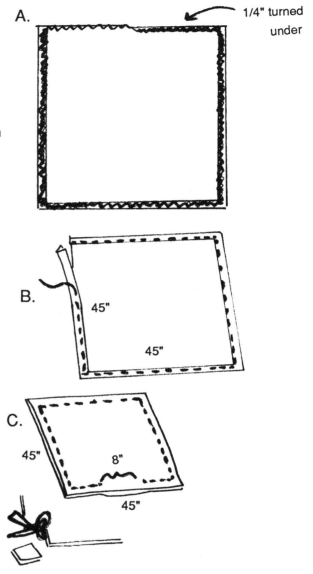

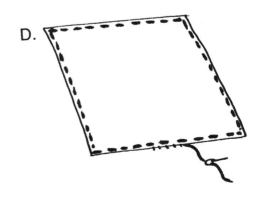

SHEETS - FITTED BOTTOM

-1 7/8 yards 45" fabric,cotton, or
  cotton T-shirting
-36" elastic 1/4" wide

Layout and Cut

A. Cut your sheet fabric 66"x41".

Sewing Directions - Corners

B. Measure and mark 7" from each corner.

C. Fold one long side to one short side
placing right sides together. Match 7"
marks. Measure 7" across fabric to fold.
(approximately 9 1/2" from point of fold to
7" mark on fold.) Stitch from edge to fold.
Cut 1/2" from seam line.

D. Repeat steps C and D for each corner.

Edges

E. Turn under 1/4" and 1/4" again on all
sides. Stitch close to inside edge.

F. Mark center of each end of the sheet.
and centers of 18" elastic strips. Pin center
of elastic to center of one end of sheet on
the wrong side of the fabric.   Pin ends of
elastic 3" past end seams.

G.   Stretch elastic while stitching.
Backstitch ends of elastic.

H. Repeat steps F. and G. for other end of sheet.

A.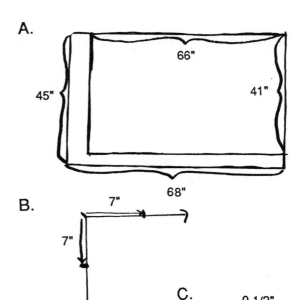

B.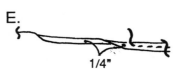

C.

E.

F.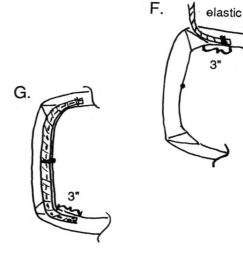

G.

TOP SHEET

-2 yards 45" fabric

Why have a top sheet! This was a great idea from Bessie Lerner who made the accessories for this book. Having a top sheet is great for warm evenings. It gives a layer of protection between baby and quilts or other blankets. It makes the crib like a regular bed. Thanks Bessie for a great idea! !

Layout and Cut

A. Cut sheet panel 45"x60". Cut strip for the header 4"x45". (This 4" strip can be from a coordinate fabric. **OR,** If you want to applique it, you may want to cut it 8" wide.)

Sewing Directions -
Finishing Sides

B. If sides of the fabric have printing in selvage, turn   it to the wrong side. Stitch close to turned under edge.

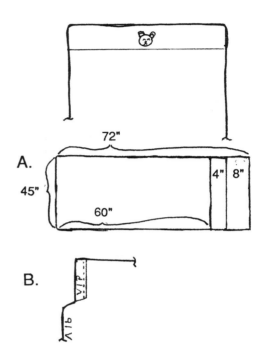

Top

C. Place the right side of this 4" strip to the wrong side of the sheet. Stitch 1/2" seam.

D. Turn top panel at seam to the right side. Turn under 1/2" on unfinished edge toward the wrong side of the fabric. Stitch close to the edge.

Bottom edge

E. Turn under 1/2" and 1/2" again to the wrong side. Stitch close to inside edge.

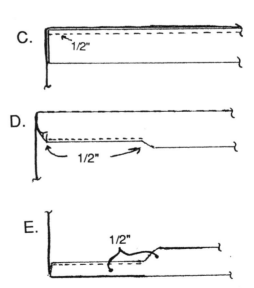

CAR SEAT COVER

This car seat cover is designed to be easy to make and fit over most of the car seats now on the market. I think you will enjoy it.

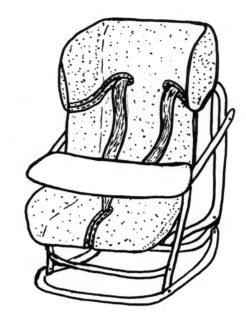

-1 bath towel- 25"x51"
-1 washcloth
-4 yards of 1/2" double fold bias tape
-2 velcro tabs

Layout and Cut

A. Cut the washcloth in half (you will have two 6 1/2" x13" pieces).

Sewing Directions

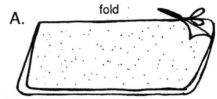

A.

B. Pin cut edge of washcloth to long edge of towel. Continue pinning together along short end of washcloth and other long side. Stitch 1/2" seam, easing around the corners. Zig zag along cut edge of washcloth.

C. Repeat Step B for other side.

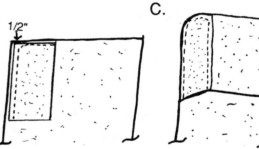

B.

C.

Safety Strap Opening

D. Put seat cover over your car seat. Mark where your straps are located directly on the towel.

E. Draw a straight line from outside edge of strap location to edge under washcloth. Cut along this line. Do this for both sides of the towel.

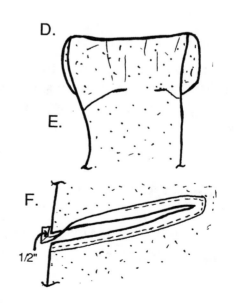

D.

E.

F. Finish cut edges by pinning 1/2" wide double fold bias tape along edge on both right and left sides. Turn under 1/2" of tape at each end to finish them. Stitch close to inside edge.

F.

Note: Some car seat covers will require an opening in the front for a center strap follow steps D - F.

CAR SEAT COVER Continued

Side Strap- Optional

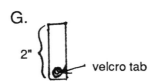

G.   Attach one portion of velcro to one end of a 2" long strip of bias tape.

H.   Attach opposite end of strip to the under side of the towel 1" from edges. Stitch across end of tape.

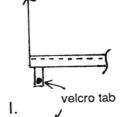

I.   Attach other portion of velcro on under side of towel to meet velcro piece on strap.

J.   Repeat Steps G-I for other side strap.

Tip: I suggest you make openings for only one set of strap openings. If preparing this cover for a small child, make openings for the lower straps. You can make openings for the upper strap openings later.

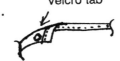

UNDER CAR SEAT MAT
protection for your cars upholstery

-1/2 yard vinyl

A.   Place this vinyl under the infant seat between the infant seat and the upholstery.

As parents we frequently give food and snacks to the children while in the car. This mat will help protect the upholstery.

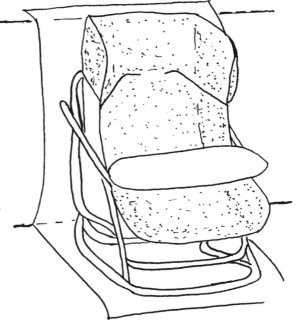

HIGH CHAIR AND ROCKER PADS

-1 yard 45" fabric
-1" thick foam pad (approximately 1 yard)

Measurements

A. This pattern is made to fit a high chair
which is 18" high (from the seat to the top
of the back) 15" wide at the top of the back
and 11" wide at the bottom of the back of
the chair. The seat is 11" wide at the back,
13" wide across the front and 11" deep.

B. PLEASE! take these measurements before
you start-to make sure your chair is close
to the same size.

Chair or rocker back:

Height ___Wide___Top___Bottom___

Chair or rocker seat:

Depth___Wide___Front___Back___

A. B.

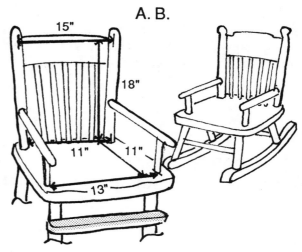

Layout and Cut - Foam Padding

C. Using 1" foam padding, mark the
dimensions onto the padding. Do marking
with a straight edge and marker. Cut out
pads along these marks. (When you mark the
foam, you mark a rectangle 18"x15" then
measure in 2" from both 18" sides on 15"
edge. Draw a line from the 2" marks to the
opposite corners.)

C.

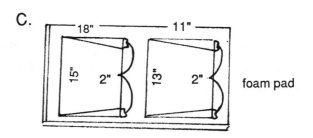

foam pad

HIGH CHAIR AND ROCKER PADS
Continued

Fabric

D. Mark the same dimensions on the fabric with tailor chalk and a straight edge. Cut 1" to the outside of the first mark to allow for the fullness of the padding.

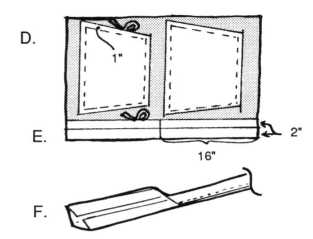

E. Cut out four strips of fabric 16" long and 2" wide.

Sewing Directions - Ties

F. Make fabric ties by folding each tie in half lengthwise. Fold each edge in to meet on pressed fold. Fold on original fold and stitch close to edge. Zig zag ends.

Assembling

G. Take back and seat panels and place them so right sides of fabric are together. Place ties in top corners of the back cover and in the back corners of the seat cover.

H. Stitch 1/2" seams leaving 8" open in back of bottom seams to allow for turning right side out. Clip corners.

I. Turn right side out. Place foam pad inside fabric. Hand stitch opening closed.

NOTE: Your may want to place extra ties in the bottom of the back pad and in the front of the seat pad. This is to your preference and can be added at any time.

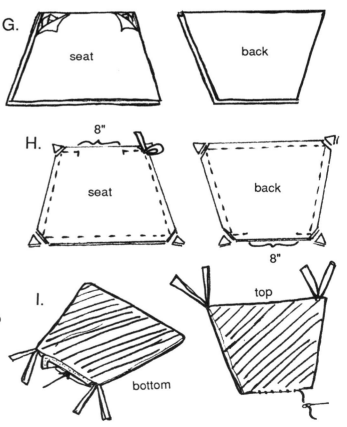

HIGH CHAIR PADDED COVER

-1 yard 45" fabric
-29"x29" batting section
-3 yards of 1/4" ribbon or make fabric ties

Layout and Cut

A. From fabric cut two 13"x14" arm panels, two 14"x29" chair panels, and ten 2"x20" ties. From batting cut two 13"x7" arm panels and one 14"x29" chair panel.

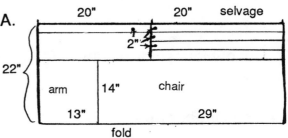

Sewing Directions - Arm Panels

B. Fold arm panels in half so you have two 13"x7" rectangles. Place batting on the bottom. Stitch 1/2" seam along 7" sides. Clip corners. Turn right side out.

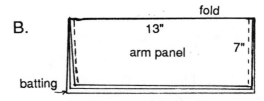

Assembling

C. Take arm panels and place them right sides together with one chair panel. (Folded edges meeting in the middle.) Both arm panels should be 1/2" from bottom end. Pin.

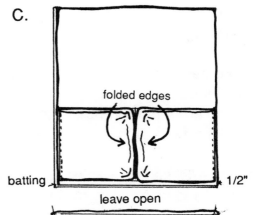

D. Place second chair panel right side to pinned arm and chair panel. Place batting on the bottom.

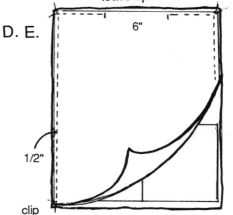

E. Stitch 1/2" seam around all edges. Please be careful not to catch arm panels in bottom seam. Leave 6" open in opposite end. Clip corners. Trim seams as needed.

F. Turn right side out. Stitch opening closed.

HIGH CHAIR PADDED COVER Continued

Ties

G.   Make fabric ties by folding each tie in half lengthwise.   Fold each edge in to meet on pressed fold.   Fold on original fold and stitch close to edge.   Zig zag ends.

H.   Fold tie-downs in half widthwise. Stitch a tie to all corners and at bottom of arm panels   (see diagram).

NOTE: For some high chairs, a standard infant seat cover will slip over the back of the chair where ties would not work.

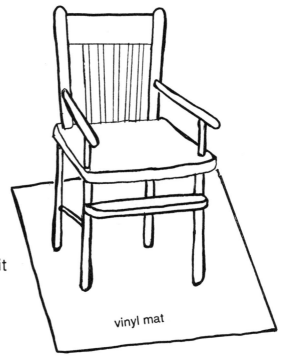

HIGH CHAIR MAT
floor   or   carpet   protection

1 yard vinyl - coordinate color with eating area.

A.   Use a yard stick to make sure edges are straight.

B.   Place this mat under your child's high chair.   Most of the food and spills will land on this mat.   After meals pick it up and throw the crumbs in the garbage and wash it off.

vinyl mat

HIGH CHAIR SECURE

This is great to take with you to make sure your child will be secure in the chairs at restaurants while you are eating. It is also super for the little ones who cannot sit up well yet.

Use your imagination in decorating it using rick rack, applique etc.

-3/4 yard of two different colors 45" fabric cotton duck, sailcloth, denim, or something easy care and sturdy
-11 feet of bias or fabric tape or ribbon

DESIGN 1 - Two different fabrics

Layout and Cut - Main color
A. Cut fabric to 18" wide making sure cut edges are straight. On left selvage, measure 6" and 12" from bottom cut edge, marking both points.

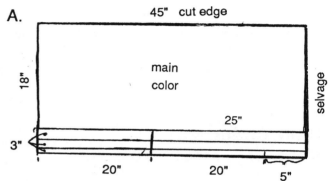

B. On cut edges, measure 10" and 10" more from left selvage marking all points on top and bottom cut edges.

C. At first 10" marks, measure in 6" and mark both points. Connect 6" marks to 6" and 12" marks on selvage (see diagram). Connect 6" marks and second 10" marks as in diagram. Cut along these lines.

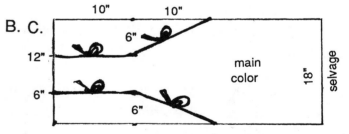

Co-ordinate Color
D. Repeat Steps A-C. Measure and mark 3" past second 10" marks on edges. Connect the 3" marks. Cut along line.

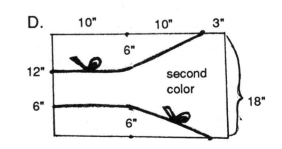

Ties
E. If not using bias tape or ribbon, cut four 3"x20" strips and two 3"x25" strips. Make fabric ties by folding each tie in half lengthwise. Fold each edge in to meet on pressed fold. Fold on original fold and stitch close to edge. Zig zag ends.

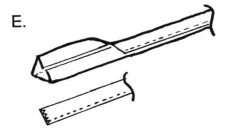

Sewing Directions - Top Edge

F. Along 18" top edges, turn under 1/2" and 1/2" again. Topstitch close to inside edge.

Assembling

G. Take two 20" ties and place at second 10" marks on each side. Pin in place.

H. Take 25" ties and pin 3/4" down from corners of 6" end strip.

I. Place contrast fabric right sides together with ties in-between. Stitch 1/2" seam around all edges, back stitch across ties.

J. Clip corners and trim seams as needed. Turn right side out. Topstitch close to all edges. Stitch across top edge of contrast fabric on back.

Back Flap

K. Fold top 18" panel down so right sides are together and top finished edge meets 3" mark. Stitch 1/2" seam from fold to 10" mark. Zig zag edge. Turn right side out. (This is the part that fits over the back of the chair.)

DESIGN 2 - One Color

-1 1/4 yard of one color 45" wide
-11 feet of bias tape, ribbon or fabric tape

Layout and Cut

B. Layout and cut as stated in steps A-D.

Sewing Directions

C. Assemble as in steps E-K.

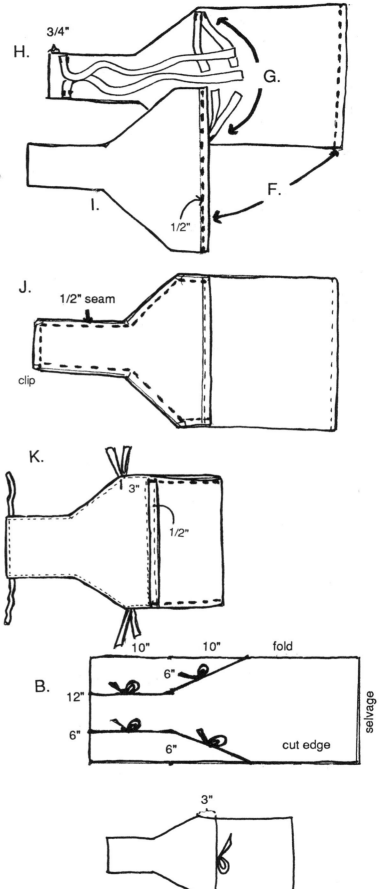

67

INFANT SEAT COVERS

Infant seat covers give a layer of comfort between baby and the vinyl pad. It helps absorb wetness and can be thrown into the wash when dirty.

This cover can also be used as a seat cover for some strollers and high chairs.

-1/2 yard fabric, use pre-quilted fabric, toweling, flannel, or heavy cotton of a light color
-3 yards of 1/2" wide double fold bias tape

Measurements

A. Measure your infant seat to make sure a 17"x27" cover will fit.

DESIGN 1 - One Layer With Tape Edge

Layout and Cut

B. Cut one piece of fabric 18"x29" for front panel and one piece 8"x18" for back panel.

Sewing Directions - Back Panel

C. Pin tape to one 18" side of back panel. Stitch close to inside edge.

D. Pin unfinished 18" edge of back panel to top of front panel so right sides are together. Stitch 1/2" seam.

Edges

E. Fold at seam so wrong sides are together. Pin bias tape to outside edges of infant seat. Begin at top seam putting both layers inside tape. Fold tape at corners. Stitch close to inside edge.

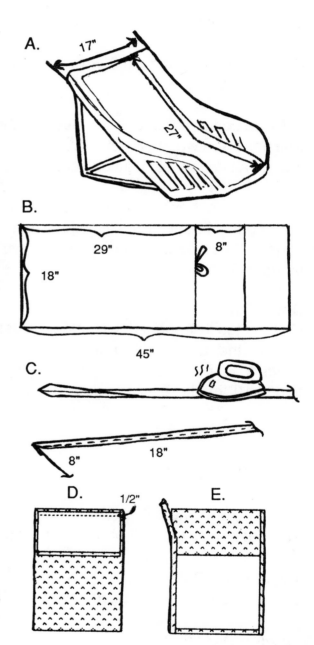

INFANT SEAT COVERS Continued

DESIGN 2 - Comforter Style With Tape Edge

-1 1/8 yard 45" fabric use pre-quilted fabric, toweling, flannel, or heavy cotton of a light color
-3 yard of 1/2" wide double fold bias tape
-batting

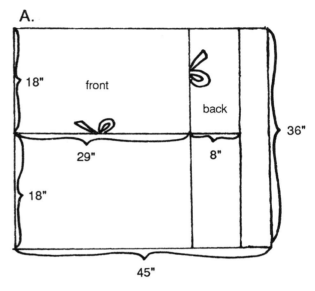

Layout and Cut

A. Cut two 18"x29" pieces for front panel and two 8"x18" pieces of fabric for back panel. Cut one of each piece from batting.

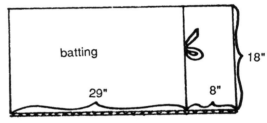

Sewing Directions

B. Place fabric pieces wrong sides together with batting between. Quilt by stitching every 3" from top to bottom or tack every 4" for a comforter effect.

C. Assemble cover beginning at Step C Design 1.

DESIGN 2 - Plain Edge

-5/8 yard of 45" fabric (for one layer cover)

Layout and Cut

A. Cut one 20"x32" seat panel and one 8"x20" back panel or add 2" to both the width and length of your infant seat measurements. Cut one of each.

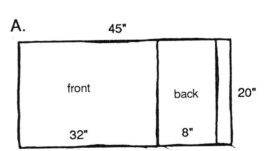

INFANT SEAT COVERS-Plain Edge
Continued

Sewing Directions

B. Place back panel right sides together with seat panel so 20" sides are together. Stitch 1/2" seam. Zig zag seam edge.

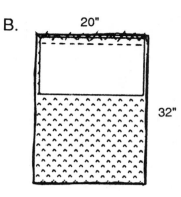

B.

20"

32"

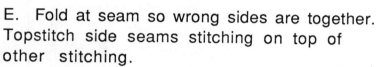

C.

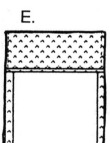

1/4"

C. Turn under 1/4" and 1/4" again on top and bottom edges. Stitch close to inside edge.

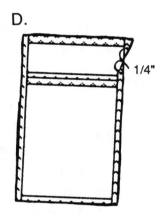

D.

1/4"

D. Turn under 1/4" and 1/4" again on side edges. Stitch close to inside edges.

E. Fold at seam so wrong sides are together. Topstitch side seams stitching on top of other stitching.

E.

NOTE: Any of these covers can be appliqued or quilted in your own design. Use your imagination and have fun.

INFANT SEAT COVER - For Seat With Curved Sides

-5/8 yard of 45" fabric use pre-quilted
  fabric, toweling, flannel, or heavy cotton
  of a light color
-26" of 1/4" elastic

Layout and Cut

A. Cut one piece of fabric 36"x20"

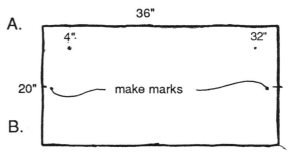

Marking

B. On both 36" edges, measure down 4" and
32" from top edge. Mark on wrong side of
fabric. Measure in 4" from each mark and
mark as in the diagram. Also mark the
center of both the top and bottom.

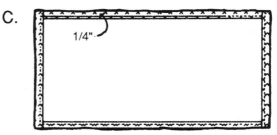

Sewing Directions

C. Turn under 1/4" and 1/4" on all edges.
Stitch close to inside edge.

D. Fold top and bottom, at 4" marks, toward
right side of fabric. Stitch from 4" marks
on fold to side edge making a dart at each
corner. (see diagram)

E. Cut elastic into two 13" pieces. Mark
center of piece. Match center of elastic to
center mark on wrong side of fabric. Pin. Pin
ends of elastic 2" past corner seams. Stitch
down center of elastic, stretching elastic
while stitching.

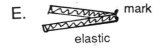

F. Repeat this step for other end of cover.

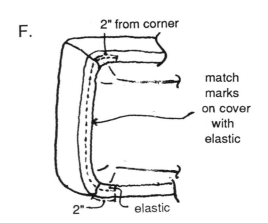

NOTE: This cover should stay in place and not come off
every time you put your baby in or take him out of the
seat.

PLAYPEN PAD

Should you need to replace your playpen pad, this is the design you need.

The average playpen is 40" square. Measure the inside bottom of yours to make sure it is the same size. If it is not, cut your fabric and padding to your measurements plus 1" for seam allowances and 1" for padding.

-2 1/2 yards 45" fabric
-quilt batting **OR** 1" thick foam pad the size of the bottom of your playpen

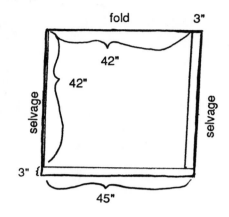

Layout and Cut - With Batting

A. Cut two 42" squares of fabric. With right sides of squares together, place batting on bottom side of fabric. (If you desire a decorative effect applique before stitching together or use rick rack, lace or ruffling in the seams.)

Sewing Directions

B. Stitch a 1/2" seam on three and a half sides. Leave approximately 12" in the middle of fourth side open to turn the pad right side out. Trim the seam and clip corners.

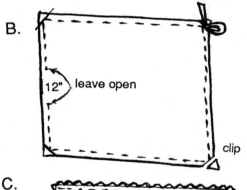

C. Turn right side out. Stitch opening closed. If desired, topstitch 1/4" from seam, machine quilt or tack every 4".

With Foam Pad

D. If you are using a 1" foam pad, follow directions above without using batting. Insert foam pad at Step C. Then stitch opeining closed.

OPTION: If you want the cover to be removable, leave one side open, zig zag raw edges of open seam. Turn under 1/2" and stitch close to inside edge.

REMOVABLE PLAYPEN PAD COVER

Made to fit 40" square playpen

-2 yards 45" fabric
-lace or ruffle (optional)

Layout and Cut

A. Cut one top panel 42" square and two bottom panels 42"x10".

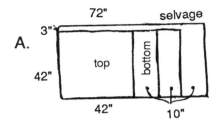

Sewing Directions - Bottom Panels

B. On one 42" edge of bottom panel turn under 1/2" and 1/2" again. Stitch close to inside edge. Repeat this step for other bottom panel.

Assembling

C. Place bottom panels right sides together with top panel so bottom panels are at opposite sides. Stitch 1/2" seam. Zig zag seams and edges of fabric between bottom panels.

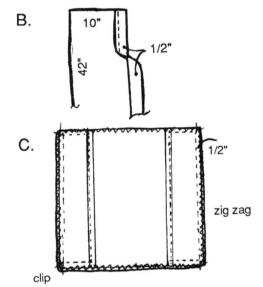

D. Clip corners, turn right side out. Fold under seam allowance between back panels. Stitch close to inside edge. Finish fabric between panels on other side in same manner.

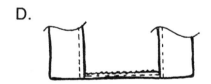

To Use

Place pad inside cover with back panels on the bottom.

STROLLER BUNTING

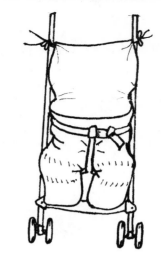

-2 yards 45" fabric
-2 20" cords
-12" zipper
-quilt batting

Layout, Cut and Mark

A. Cut 2 back panels 18"x40" and two front panels 18"x29". Cut one of each from batting.

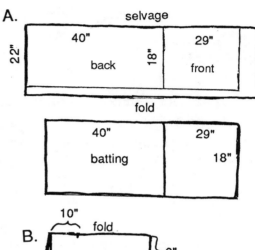

Leg slit

B. Lay the front panels wrong sides together with batting in the middle. Fold in half lengthwise. Mark the center of bottom edge. Measure 10" from the bottom on fold. Make a mark. Connect these marks. Cut a slit between them.

C. Repeat this step for back panels. Then measure down 11" from top edge on sides. Mark each side.

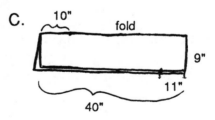

Sewing Directions - Back Panel

D. Place back panels right sides together with batting on the bottom. Stitch 1/2" seam beginning at the 11" mark on one side. Stitch to the top, across and down to the 11" mark on the other side.

E. Clip corners turn right side out.

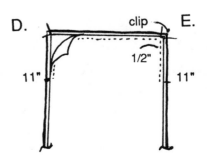

Front Panel

F. Place front panels right sides together with batting on the bottom. Stitch 1/2" seam across top. Clip away batting. Turn right side out.

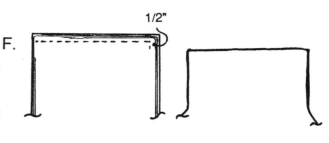

Zipper

G. Place zipper face down on the right edge of the back panel. Place tabs at 11" mark. Stitch down the middle of the right side of zipper.

H. Place left edge of zipper on left front edge of front panel. Stitch down center of the left side of the zipper.

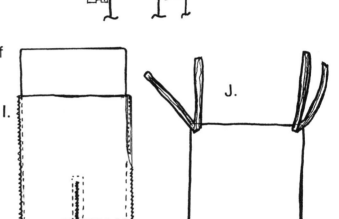

Finishing

I. Place right sides together. Stitch 1/2" seam around bottom of bunting. Zig zag edge. Clip corners, turn right side out.

Ties

J. Take 20" cords, fold them in half, stitch fold onto bunting at the back top corners. Stitch across the fold and through all layers of the bunting.

STROLLER RAIN COVER

-1 1/4 yard 60" water repellent or water
  resistant fabric
-9" zipper
-1/4" elastic
-1/2" wide double fold bias tape
-6"x6" piece of firm interfacing

Layout and Cut

A. Cut cover fabric 23"x45", cut hood fabric
18"x9". Cut two 5"x10" zipper covers
(narrow one 5" end to 3".)

B. On cover panel, measure 4" from each
corner in each direction. Mark each point.

C. Fold panel in half lengthwise. Cut along
fold then measure 14", 23", and 32" from
top. Mark each point.

Sewing Directions - Zipper

D. Place panels right sides together. Stitch
from bottom to 23" mark.

E. Open seam, place zipper between 23" and
32" marks so tabs are at 23" mark. Stitch
down both sides and across bottom. Undo
stitching in seam in front of zipper.

Hood

F. Fold hood pieces right sides together.
Stitch 1/2" seam from fold to opposite edge.
Zig zag edge.

G. Zig zag opposite edge of hood panel. Turn
under 1/2". Stitch close to inside edge.

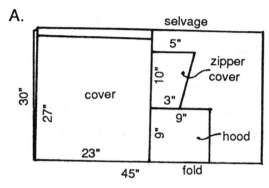

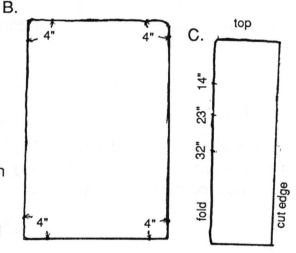

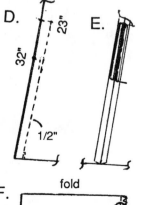

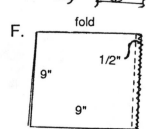

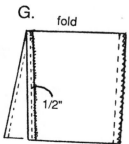

STROLLER RAIN COVER Continued

Assembling

H. Stitch 1/2" seam from top edge to 14" mark.

I. Place hood panel right sides together with cover panel matching seam of hood to seam on cover panel. Stitch 1/2" seam. Zig zag edge.

Corners

J. At one corner, fold right sides together matching 4" marks. Stitch from 4" marks to fold about 4 1/2" from corner point. Cut 1/2" from stitching. Zig zag edge.

K. Repeat this for other three corners.

Outside Edges

L. Zig zag around outside edges.

M. Turn under 1/2" to wrong side. Stitch close to inside edge.

Elastic

N. Pin center of elastic to center of top on the wrong side. Pin ends 4" past corner seam. Stitch down center of elastic while stretching it to fit.

O. Repeat for bottom.

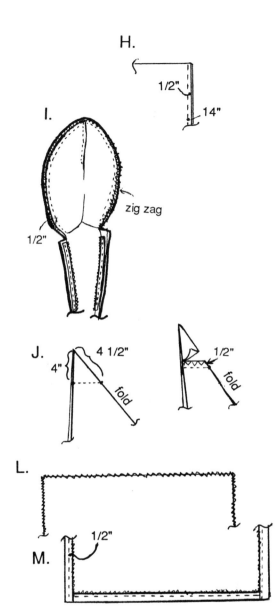

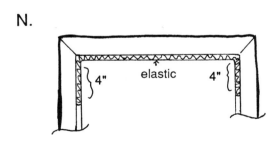

Zipper Cover

P. Place right sides together. Stitch 1/2"
seam around all edges leaving 4" open in
middle of one side. Clip corners, trim seams.

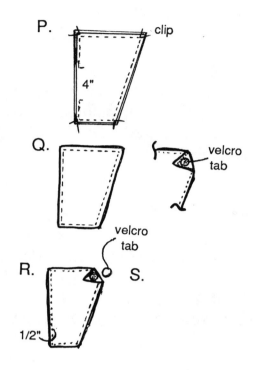

Q. Turn right side out. Stitch close to
edges. Stitch 1 portion of velcro tab to the
under side of top right corner.

R. Place straight edge of zipper cover 1/2"
to the left of the zipper so it will flap over
the zipper. Stitch close to left edge.

S. Stitch other velcro tab on the cover
opposite to the first tab.

To Use

When raining, after placing your baby in the
stroller, place this cover over him to keep
him dry. The top should fit over the top
back. The bottom should fit under the
bottom foot panel. Pull the sides of the
cover over the sides of the stroller. Enjoy
your stroll in the rain! ! ! Your baby will.

STROLLER SHOPPING BAG FOR FULL ARM STANDARD STROLLER

-1 yard 45" fabric
-18" of 1/4" elastic

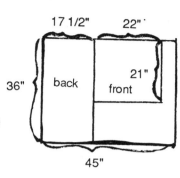

Layout and Cut

A. Cut one piece of fabric 36"x17 1/2" for back of bag and one piece 21"x22" for front of bag. (If your stroller bar is wider than 16" add two inches to your measurement instead of the 17 1/2" measurement above.)

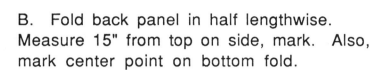

B. Fold back panel in half lengthwise. Measure 15" from top on side, mark. Also, mark center point on bottom fold.

Sewing Directions - Front Panel

C. On one 22" side of front panel, mark center bottom of panel.

D. On other 22" side, turn under 1/2" and 1/2" again making a casing. Topstitch close to inside edge.

E. Ease 18" of elastic through casing.

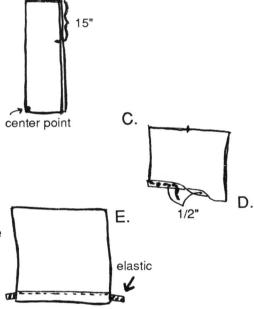

Assembling

F. Take unfinished bottom edge of front panel, match side edges and center bottom mark with back panel.

G. Fold under the extra fabric on each side of center point so there is approximately 1" on each side (or just gather the bottom).

H. Stitch 1/2" seam around front panel. Clip corners

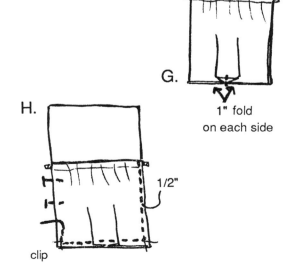

Top Flap

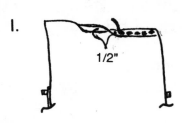

I. At top of back panel, turn under 1/2" and 1/2" again to side away from pocket. Stitch close to inside edge.

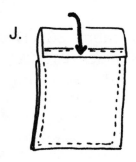
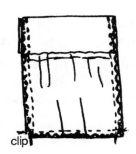

J. Fold finished edge down to meet pocket on opposite side of fabric. Zig zag edges.

K. Clip corners. Turn pocket top right side out. The top should be on the opposite side of pocket.

NOTE: You may want to add a tie at each bottom corner. Why? Should your bag get heavy, the strap can be tied around the bottom poles of the stroller so it won't tip up.

Ties

A. Take two 14" pieces of cord or 1/2" wide double fold bias tape. (Stitch open edge closed).

B. Stitch mid-point of one tie to one bottom corner of the bag. Repeat this for other strap.

C. Finish ends with fray check or zig zag.

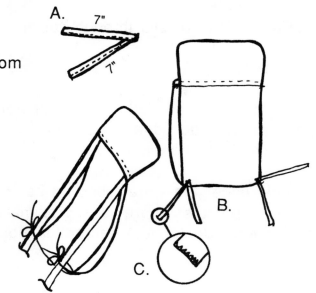

STROLLER SHOPPING BAG (UMBRELLA)

-3/4 yard 45" fabric
-14" of 1/4" elastic

Layout and Cut

A. Cut one piece 14"x22" and one piece 21" x 22".

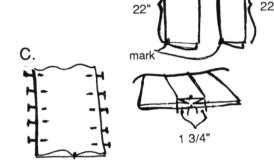

B. Fold both pieces in half lengthwise. Mark fold point on bottom of each piece.

Sewing Directions

C. With right sides together, match dots. Match outside edges pinning sides. Fold extra material so 1 3/4" of fabric is on each side of dot. (You're making a pleat). **OR** just gather the bottom edge.

D. Stitch 1/2" seam down one side, across bottom, and up other side. Zig zag edge.

E. At top of bag, turn under 1/2" and 1/2" again. Stitch close to inside edge leaving 1" open at side seams.

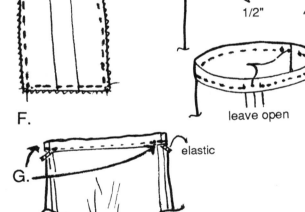

F. Ease 14" elastic through 21" side of bag.

G. Stitch through elastic and fabric casing at each seam.

H. Take two strips 1x6" long (made from fabric tape, bias tape, or ribbon), fold in half widthwise. Stitch to back 14" panel at top corners.

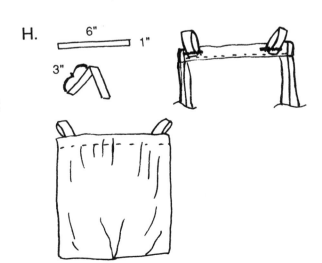

OPTION: Add ties as described in Standard Stroller Shopping Bag page 76.

UMBRELLA STROLLER COVER

-3/4 yard 45" or 36" fabric
-4 heavy weight snaps or 4 strips of velcro
    or eight 6" pieces of cord

NOTE: The **standard stroller** cover is made the same way as the infant seat cover on page 68.

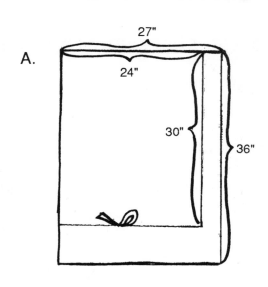

A.

Layout and Cut

A. Cut one piece of fabric 30"x24".

Sewing Directions - Outside Edges

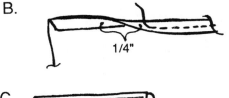

B.

B. Turn under 1/4" and 1/4" again on all sides. Stitch close to inside edges on all sides.

Marking - Side Darts

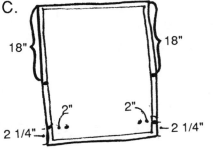

C.

C. Measure down 18" on both 30" sides, mark. Measure up 2 1/4" from bottom on both sides, mark. Measure in 2" from 2 1/4" marks on side.

D. Match 18" marks on edge to marks 2" from side edges.

Sewing Directions

E. Measure 8 1/2" on the fold you made, make mark, then stitch seam from 8 1/2" mark to matched marks on edge.

F. Place top of snaps, velcro piece or tie on wrong side of fabric in each corner. Place bottom pieces 2 1/2" to the middle along edge on wrong side of fabric.

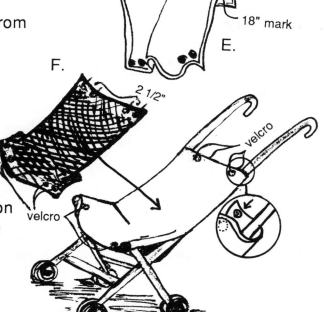

D.
E.
F.

BONNET

Made from a hanky and to be cherished
forever. MANY thanks to Sylvia Stogdon.

MAGIC HANKIE

I'm just a little hanky as square as square can be. But with a
stitch or two they made a bonnet out of me. You wear me from the
hospital and on your dedication day. Then I'll be neatly pressed
and just as neatly packed away.

And on your happy wedding day I'm sure you will be told, that
every well dressed bride will wear an article that is old. It would
be very fitting if on that happy day to be. If you will snip some
stitches so I'd once again be me.

And if by chance you are a boy, on some fine day you'll wed.
Please give your bride this hanky once worn upon your head.

Materials

-one 10" handkerchief or fabric 11"x11"
-40" of rick rack or lace
-24" ribbon tie

Sewing Directions -
From Fabric

Edges

A. Turn under 1/4" and 1/4" again on all
edges. Stitch close to turned under edge.

A.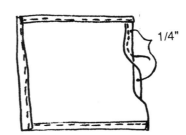
1/4"

Option: To decorate the fabric use rick rack, lace or
embroider all edges of fabric.

B.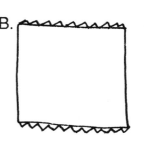
OPTION:

C.
1/4"

Back Gathering Casing

C. Fold fabric in half so wrong sides are
together. Stitch 1/4" from fold using a
large basting stitch making a casing.

BONNET Continued

D. Insert heavy duty thread into 1/4" casing.
Pull thread and gather fabric completely.
Tie thread in a knot.

Ties

E. Turn under 1/4" of ribbon on each end of
ties to wrong side. Stitch ribbon to corners
through both layers.

OPTION: If desired, embroider or applique a design on
one side.

**Sewing Directions -
From Handkerchief**

Follow steps above beginning at Step B.

This bonnet makes a very special gift.

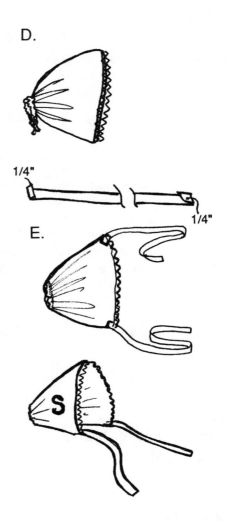

D.

1/4"

1/4"

E.

S

BOTTLE SOCK

-9"x7" piece of fabric
-6" of 1/4" elastic

Sewing Directions - Top Edge

A. Press under 1/2" then 1/2" to the wrong side on one 9" edge. Stitch close to each edge.

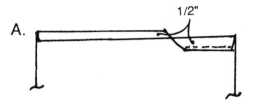

A.

B. Insert 6" of 1/4" elastic into the casing made. Pin edges of elastic to hold in place.

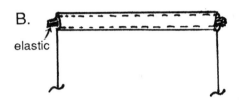

B.
elastic

Assembling

C. Fold right sides together. Stitch 1/4" seam down side and across bottom. Zig zag edge.

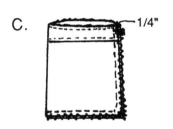

C. 1/4"

Bottom Corners

D. Fold bottom to side seam. Measure 1" from top of seam on each fold you made; mark. Stitch between marks.

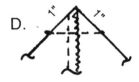

D.

E. Repeat step D for other end of bottom seam and side fold.

E.

F. Turn right side out. Put a bottle into the sock.

F.

OPTIONS: Stitch rick-rack or lace around top of edge before inserting elastic. **OR** Applique a decorative design on fabric before assembling. **OR** Embroider the name of the baby on the sock.

BUNTINGS

DESIGN 1 - Large Bunting with Rounded Tie Hood

-2 yard 36" or 45" fabric (If you use pre-quilted
 fabric only one yard is needed. If using a pre-printed
 square, fold it in half lengthwise so design is in middle of
 back panel. Make sure quilting has cotton on both sides.
 Fabric with cotton on both sides is preferred.)
-22" zipper
-45" of 1" wide double fold bias tape
-5 1/2 feet cord 1/4" wide

Layout and Cut

A. On fold, measure up 22", 25", 27", 32" and
34", mark each point. Measure 17 1/2" along
bottom from fold, mark.

B. Mark each of the following measurements
from marks on fold:

At 22" mark, measure 17 1/2" toward cut edge,
25"	13"
27"	11"
32"	9"
34"	5 1/2"
36"	

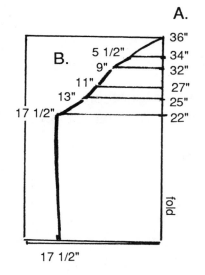

Connect marks as in diagram. Cut along lines
marked by connecting marks rounding top from
36" mark on fold to 5 1/2" mark.

C. Lay this design on top of fabric. Pin and
cut second panel.

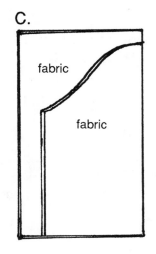

D. Lay these on top of batting, folds
together. Cut one layer of batting.

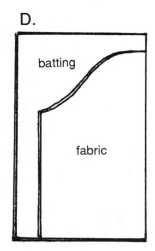

86

BUNTINGS - DESIGN 1 Continued

Quilting

E. Place fabric panels wrong side together with batting between. Stitch from top to bottom every 2 or 3".

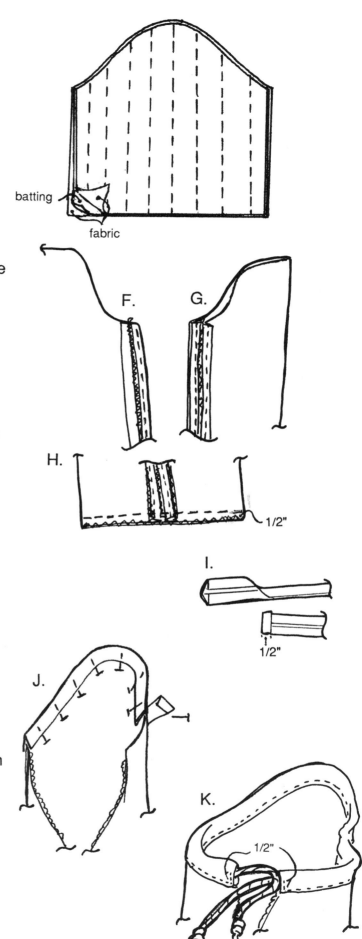

Sewing Directions

F. Take the zipper, place it face down on the right edge on the right side of the fabric. Stitch down center of right side of zipper.

G. Fold fabric in half placing right sides together. Place unstitched half of zipper on left selvage. Stitch down center of left side of zipper. Zig zag the edges of the zipper to raw edges.

Bottom Seam

H. With right sides together, match zipper with center back fold. Stitch 1/2" seam across bottom of fabric. Zig zag edge.

Hood Finish

I. Take 45"x2" fabric strip, fold sides in to meet in the middle; fold again. Turn under 1/2" at end of fabric tape.

J. Pin tape to hood. Turn under 1/2" at both ends of tape. Stitch close to open edge making a casing.

K. At front edge, stitch 1/2" from bottom edge of tape up. Pull cord through top casing. Tie knots in each end of cord.

BUNTINGS Continued

Design 2 - Small Bunting with Rounded Hood

-28"x30" rectangle or
  1 pre-quilted fabric square as stated in
  Design 1
-18" zipper
-39" of 1" wide double fold bias tape
-5 ft. of 1/4" wide cord

Layout and Cut

B. On fold, measure up 18", 20", 22", 27",
and 30", mark each point.

At 18" mark, measure 14" toward selvage:
20"	13"
22"	10"
27"	7"
30"	5"

Connect marks as in diagram. Cut out along
lines made by connecting the marks.

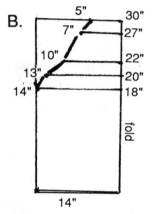
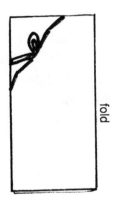

C. Assemble as described in Design 1.

Variation 1 - Applique
Use the measurements from Design 1 or 2.

-2 yards cotton fabric
-1 yard quilt batting
-1" wide double fold bias tape
-zipper
-scrap material for applique design of your
  choice.

88

BUNTINGS - Applique Continued

Layout and Cut - Applique

A. Cut the design of your choice from scrap material.

Bunting

B. Cut two of each piece from fabric and one of each piece from quilt batting. Use measurements given in Design 1 or 2.

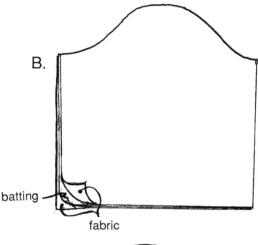

Sewing Directions

C. Pin and glue the applique design onto the right side of one bunting panel. Place non-woven tear-away interfacing on the bottom. Stitch around the design to keep it in place. Then use a close together medium wide satin zig zag stitch to finish around the design. The closer the stitches are together the richer the finished look.

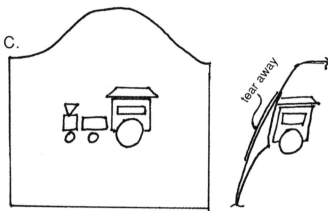

Quilting

D. Place applique panel wrong sides together with other bunting panel with batting in the middle. Pin around the applique then stitch around the outside of the applique to keep all the layers together. *To emphasize the applique and keep the batting and fabric in place, stitch every 2" or 3 " out from the applique.

E. Assemble bunting as in directions for Design 1.

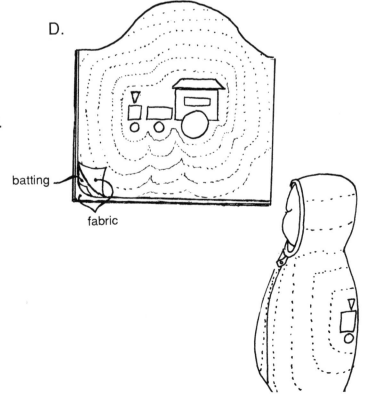

Variation 2 - Quilt Yourself
Use the measurements from Design 1 or 2.

If you like quilting and want to make your own quilt
design for your bunting you need:

-35"x31" finished design
-1 fabric panel 35"x31"(for lining)
-quilt batting 35"x31"
-1" wide double fold bias tape

Layout and Cut

A. Make your own quilt design so you have
one 35"x31" piece.

B. Use the measurements from Design 1 or
2. Cut bunting from both layers of fabric
and from one layer of quilt batting.

Sewing Directions

C. Lay your quilt design wrong sides
together with batting in the middle. Quilt
bunting around your design and through all
layers.

D. Assemble bunting as in directions for
Design 1.

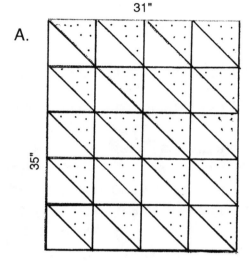

A.

31"

35"

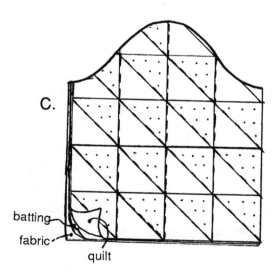

C.

batting

fabric

quilt

BURP PAD
DESIGN 1 - Plain Edge

-1/4 yard 36" or 45" quilting or flannel
-quilt batting (optional)

Layout and Cut

A. Cut two pieces of fabric 18" long and 8" wide. Mark middle of each side.

Marking

B. Measure 1" in from side mark and make another mark. Cut from one end into 1" mark and out to other end. This gives a little curve for the neck.

Sewing Directions

C. Place right sides together. Stitch 1/2" seam around all sides leaving 3" open on one side to turn right side out. Curve around edges instead of making sharp corners. Clip curves.

D. Turn right side out. Stitch opening closed. If desired, topstitch close to outside edge.

DESIGN 2 - Quilted with Tape Edge

Layout, Cut and Mark
A. Layout and cut as in step A and B above.

Assembling
B. Place fabric panels wrong sides together with batting in the middle and quilt it.

C. Finish edges using 1/2" wide double fold bias tape. Stitch close to inside edge.

OPTION: Applique or embroider a design or name onto one fabric panel. Before assembling pad.

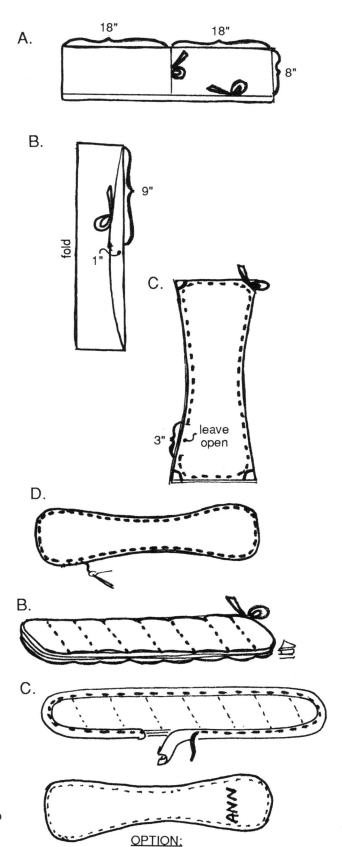

A.

18"   18"   8"

B.

fold   9"   1"

C.   3"   leave open

D.

B.

C.

OPTION:

91

DIAPER TOTE BAG WITH CHANGING PAD

DESIGN 1 - Two Layers of Fabric with Batting

-1 3/4 yard of one fabric or one yard each of
  two coordinating fabrics
-quilt batting

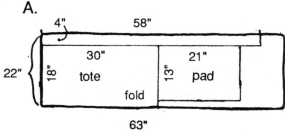

A.

Layout and Cut

A. Cut two 18"x30" tote panels, two
13"x21" changing pad panels, and two 4"x58"
strap panels from fabric. **FROM BATTING**
Cut one tote panel and one pad panel.

NOTE: one way design

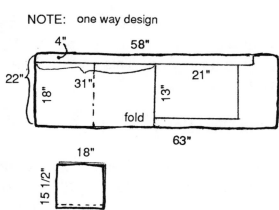

NOTE: If your fabric has a definite <u>one way design</u>, cut
bag panels 31" instead of 30" long. Cut them in half,
making four 18"x15 1/2" panels. Place two panels right
sides together so the bottom of the design is going toward
the bottom seam.

Sewing Directions - Straps

B. Connect straps by laying them right sides
together. Stitch 1/2" seam along short (4")
edges.

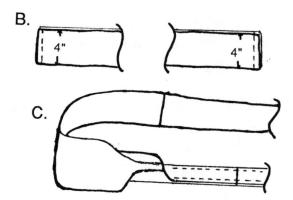

B.

C. Open strap out -they should be connected
to make one large circle. Fold sides under
1/2" then fold in half. Stitch close to both
edges.

C.

Strap to Bag

D. Place bag panels wrong sides together with
batting in the middle. Stitch around outside
edge of panel. Fold bag in half widthwise,
make a mark 3" from each edge on bottom fold.
Match outside edge of strap with 3" marks on
bottom fold. Pin strap in place.

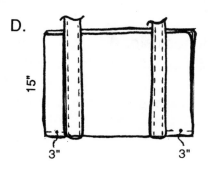

D.

DIAPER TOTE BAG Continued

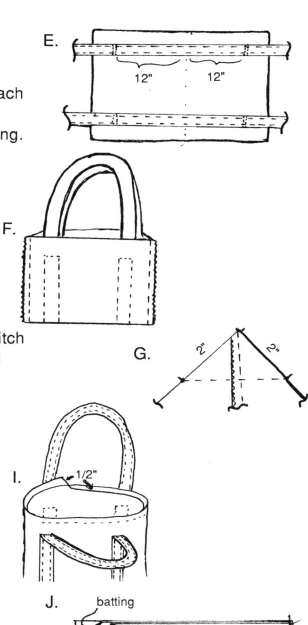

E. On straps, measure 12" each direction from mark on bottom fold. Mark and pin each point. Stitch strap to tote across the 12" marks, and on top of original strap stitching. Backstitch at 12" marks.

Stitching Bag

F. Fold tote in half with right sides together. Stitch 1/2" seam along outside edges. Zig zag the edge.

G. At corners, fold bottom seam to meet side seam. measure 2" up from point. Stitch from fold edge across seams to other fold edge. Repeat this for other corner.

H. Turn right side out.

Top Edge

I. Around top of bag, turn under 1/2" and 1/2" again. Stitch close to turned under edge.

Changing Pad

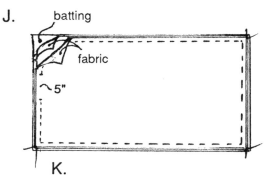

J. Place pad panels right sides together with batting on the bottom. Stitch 1/2" seam around 3 1/2 sides leaving 5" open in the middle of one side.

K. Clip corners, trim seams, turn right side out.

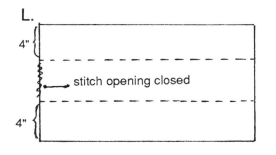

L. Stitch opening closed. To keep batting from shifting, stitch top to bottom 4" from each edge.

OPTION: Place an applique design on the front of the bag.

DIAPER TOTE BAG   Continued

DESIGN 2 - From Pre-Quilted Fabric

-1 yard pre-quilted fabric
-1/2 yard coordinate fabric
-quilt batting

Layout and Cut

A. **From pre-quilted fabric** cut one
18"x30" tote panel, two 4"x45" and two
4"x13" panels for straps. **From fabric** cut
two 13"x21" changing pad panels. **From
batting** cut one changing pad panel.

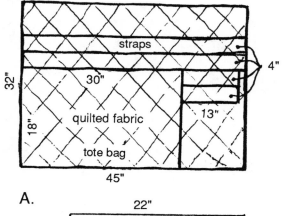

A.

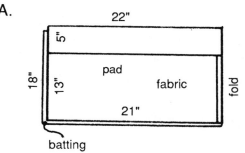

Sewing Directions

B. Assemble straps, attach to bag, and finish
bag as stated in **Design One** steps B. - I.

C. Make changing pad as stated in steps J.-L.

Grow-With-Me Idea:

Though you don't need the diapers anymore, your child can
use the bag when he spends the night with Grandma. Use it
as a beach tote. Or put your knitting, crochet, or
cross-stitch in it. If you make this out of sturdy fabric it
will last ! Mine has held up through three children.

LOVING ARMS HEADHOLDER

I designed this for my third child and loved it. It kept his head from bobbing side to side and his body from slipping.

Materials
-3/8 yard white broadcloth
-1/4 yard for tie
-1/4 yard for arm
-see diaper toppers page 29-34 for face applique
-1/4 yard interfacing
-fiberfill
-fabric glue stick

Layout and Cut
A. Cut 2 back panels 10"x12", 2 bow ties 12"x6", 1 arm panel 38"x6", and the applique pieces for the design you want as stated on the pattern. Cut only one face piece. Ears are attached later and are not appliqued.

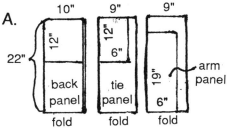

Face- Applique
B. Glue animal face onto one back panel using fabric glue stick. Position the design so you leave 4" at the bottom of the design and 1" at the top.

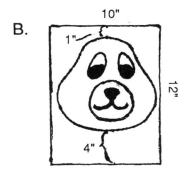

C. Place interfacing to the wrong side of one back panel. Use a basting zig zag stitch to position the pieces and keep them from slipping around the design. Then satin stitch around the design. The closer your zig zag is the richer the finished look.

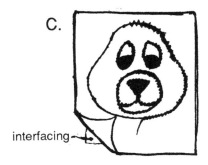

interfacing

Assembly - Back Panel
D. Place appliqued panel right side together with other back panel. If desired, place a layer of quilt batting on the bottom to the back of the applique panel. Stitch 1/2" seam around all edges leaving 4" open in the middle of one side. Clip corners and trim seam as needed.

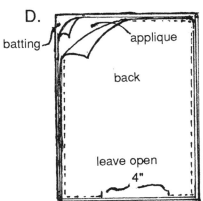

batting

applique

back

leave open 4"

E. Turn right side out, stitch opening closed Topstitch close to edge along all sides.

E.

Arms

F. Take arm panel, fold lengthwise so right sides are together. Stitch 1/2" seam along long edge. Turn right-side out.

F.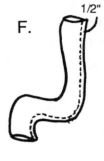

G. Fold in half to find mid-point of arms. Mark center on both edges. On one edge measure 2" each direction from center mark, make a mark.

G.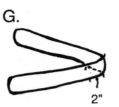

H. Place arms under face with 3 dot edge toward the bottom. Stitch between center dots.

H.

I. Fold dots on bottom to meet at center forming an upside down **V** with the arms. Stitch along both folds you formed.

I.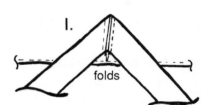
folds

Bow Tie

J. Place tie pieces wrong sides together, fold in half lengthwise and widthwise. Measure 1" up side fold from cut edge. Mark. Cut from 1" mark to selvage corner at opposite end. Stitch 1/2" seam leave 3" open on <u>each</u> end. Clip corners. Turn right side out.

J.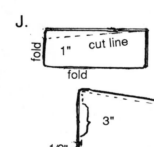

K. Fold tie in half lengthwise and widthwise again mark the center fold. Measure 1" from side fold along top fold, make a mark on both folds.

K.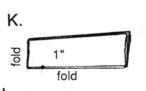

L. Unfold widthwise (it is still folded lengthwise). Stitch 1/2" from fold between 1" marks.

L.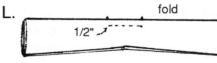

M. Open tie to lay flat, press the fold to meet the bottom stitching.

M.

LOVING ARMS HEADBOARD Continued

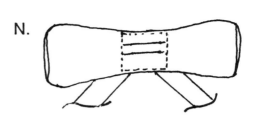

N.

N. Lay tie onto back panel under animal face and on top of arms **V** section. Stitch sides down. Stitch across top of tie to 1" marks down, across and up between marks making a square.

Ears

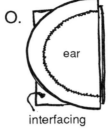

O.

ear

interfacing

O. Place inside ear piece on outer ear, glue in place; place interfacing to the wrong side of the ear and then zig zag around inside ear piece. Repeat this for other ear.

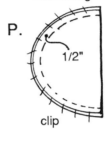

P.

1/2"

clip

P. Place ear pieces right sides together. Stitch 1/2" seam around ear; leave open where you would attach ears to head. Clip seams as needed. Turn right side out.

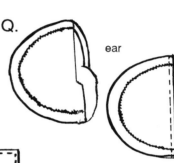

Q.

ear

Q. Fill with fiberfill. Turn under unfinished edge. Stitch opening closed.

Finishing

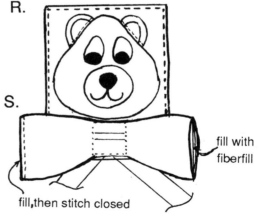

R.

S.

fill with fiberfill

fill, then stitch closed

R. Place ears on side of head at marks. Stitch close to inside edge. (They will be floppy.)

S. Put fiberfill into the ends of the tie packing fairly firm. Stitch openings closed.

T. Fill arms with fiberfill. Leave 3" at the end empty. Stitch close to stuffing.

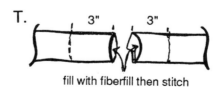

T.

3"   3"

fill with fiberfill then stitch

U. Turn under 1/2" on the end of one arm. Place other arm into this first arm. Stitch close to folded edge.

To Use - Place headholder in infant seat, car seat or swing so back of childs head rests between tie. Tie holds baby's head in position while the arms help keep baby upright in seat.

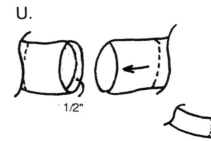

U.

1/2"

PUDDLE PADS

-1 yard 36" waterproof padding (if not available in your fabric store, check National Mail Order Catalogs)

Mattress Cover and Puddle Pads

A. Cut 14" from length of pad so you have one strip 22"x36" and one strip 14"x36".

Use the 22"x36" pad between the sheet and the crib mattress cover. This is more comfortable for the baby and saves you from washing the mattress cover everytime the baby leaks through.

The remaining 14"x36" strip can be made into lap pads or cradle/bassinet pads.

Cradle/Bassinet Pads

B. If using remaining 14"x36" strip, cut it in half widthwise so you have two 14"x18" strips. Use them in the cradle or bassinet in the same manner as you would the mattress pad.

C. If you are using the full 36"x36" pad, mark off 12", 24" on one side and 18" across the top. One yard of waterproof fabric will make six 12"x18" pads.

Lap Pads

D. If using remaining 14"x36" strip, along 36" side, mark every 12". You will make three 14"x12" pads from the remnant

E. If using a 36"x36" pad, mark every 12" on each side. You will make nine lap pads from one yard of this padding.

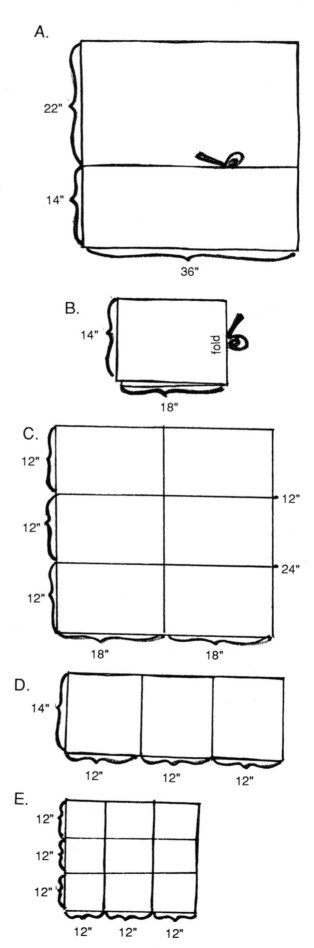

98

ROLL-UP BUMPERS

DESIGN 1 - Basic Design
-1 1/2 yards 45" fabric
-24" of cord or ribbon

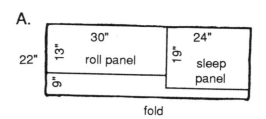

Layout and Cut

A. Cut two 19"x24" sleep panels and two 13"x30" roll panels.

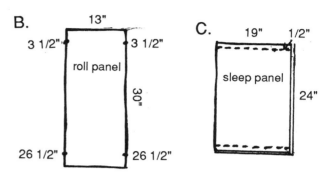

Marking

B. Measure 3 1/2" and 26 1/2" from top edge on both side edges of center panels, mark both points.

Sewing Directions
C. Place sleep panels right sides together. Stitch 1/2" seam on both 19" sides.

D. Turn right side out. Stitch close to finished edge.

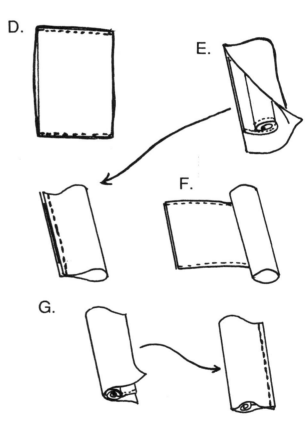

Sleep Panel to Roll Panels
E. Roll sleep panel and place it between marks inside roll panel that is folded in half with right sides together. Stitch 1/2" seam.

F. Pull panel from inside bumper tube.

G. Roll attached panels and place both panels between marks of other bumper panel that has been folded in half lengthwise with right sides together. Stitch 1/2" seam.

H. Pull attached panels from inside tube.

Ends of Tubes
I. Turn under 1/4" then 1/2" on both ends of both tubes. Stitch close to turned under edge. Leave 1" open to insert cord/ribbon.

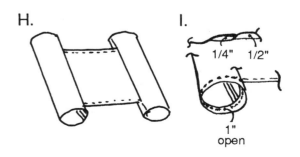

ROLL-UP BUMPERS Continued

J. Insert cord or ribbon into casing made.

K. Insert rolled batting or 4" foam circles into tubes. Pull cords and tie in bow. Push bow to inside of tube.

DESIGN 2 - Removable Roll Pads
You are making two covers for the rolled bumper using them as inserts. You can pull them out when you want to wash the sleep panel.

Layout and Cut
A. Layout and cut as above plus cut out two 28"x13" cover panels.

Sewing Directions
B. Assemble as above to step I, stitching entire edge.

Bumper Cover
C. Take tube fabric 28"x13" and fold right sides together. Stitch 1/2" along length.

D. On each end, turn under 1/4" then 1/2". Stitch close to inside edge, leaving open 1" to insert a narrow cord on each end.

E. Insert the cord in one end, pull it tight to close the end. Pull tie to inside

F. Repeat steps C-E for other bumper cover.

G. Roll 24" wide batting to the thickness you desire. (Some people may like them firmer so use more batting for a firmer bumper.) Insert batting into each cover.

H. Close the other end of each cover, tie cord, then pull it to the inside .

I. Insert covered bumper pads into bumper tubes.

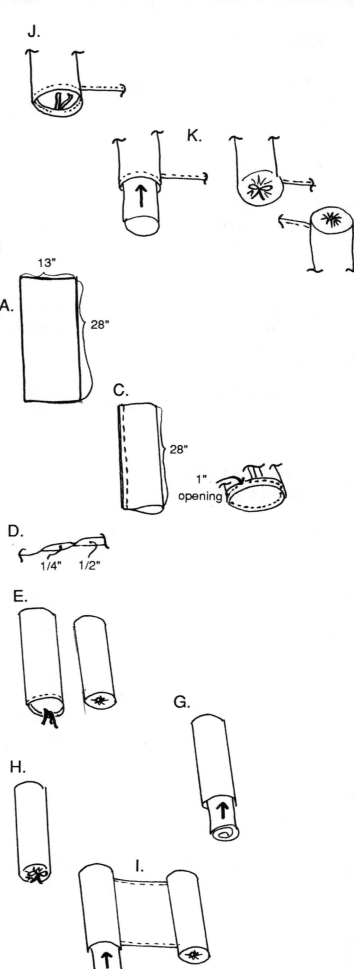

100

WALLHANGING - BALLOONS

Make several balloons and place them in a cluster on your wall. See **Variations** for **Hearts** for other ideas.

-3/8 yard of 45" fabric will make two balloons
-3/8 yard of 22" wide interfacing to make two balloons
-quilt batting
-3" of cord or ribbon
-1 yard of 1/4" wide ribbon for two balloons

Layout, Cut and Mark

A. Place balloon pattern on folded fabric. Pin in place. Add 1/2" to the outside of the pattern. Cut four balloon pieces, two from interfacing and four from batting.

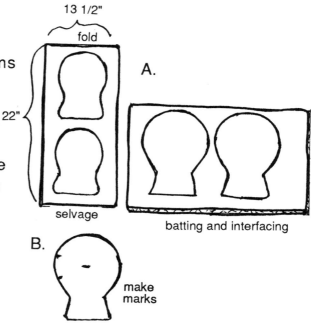

A.

selvage

batting and interfacing

B. Mark dots where you will leave it unstitched to turn right side out, mark for hanging loop and gathering lines.

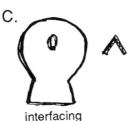

B.

make marks

Sewing Directions - Hanging Loop

C. Fold cord in half widthwise. Place cut ends on hanging mark on balloon. Place interfacing on the wrong side of the balloon Stitch across cord several times.

C.

interfacing

Assembling Balloons

D. Place balloons right sides together with batting next to the panel. Stitch 1/2" seam. leaving open between marks.

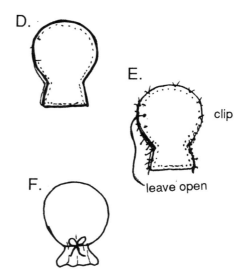

D.

E. Trim seams especially the batting. Clip curved edges and corners. Turn right side out. Stitch opening closed.

E.

clip

leave open

F. Tie 18" of ribbon around neck of balloon in a bow. Tack ribbon in place at each side.

F.

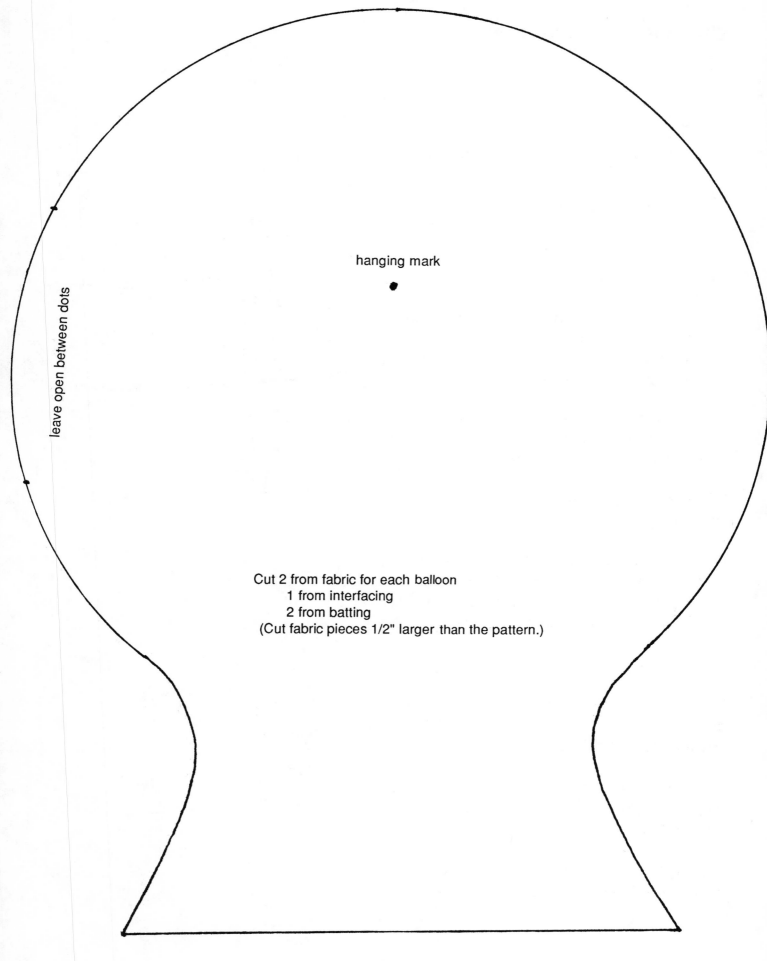

leave open between dots

hanging mark

Cut 2 from fabric for each balloon
    1 from interfacing
    2 from batting
(Cut fabric pieces 1/2" larger than the pattern.)

WALLHANGING HEARTS

Make several hearts and place them in a cluster on your wall. See **Variations** for other ideas.

-1/2 yard fabric (use coordinates to your crib items) **OR** two 12" squares
-12" square of interfacing per heart
-quilt batting
-3" of cord or ribbon

DESIGN 1 - One color
Layout, Cut and Mark

A. Place heart on fold of fabric. Pin in place. Cut 1/2" to the outside of the pattern. Cut two hearts from fabric and one or two from batting.

B. On one heart panel mark where you will leave it unstitched to turn right side out and hanging loop mark .

Sewing Directions - Hanging Loop

C. Fold cord in half widthwise. Place cut ends on hanging mark on heart. Place interfacing on the wrong side of the heart. Stitch across cord several times. Zig zag ends of loop if desired to keep them from fraying.

Assembling heart

D. Place hearts right sides together with batting next to the panel. Place this side to the bottom when stitching 1/2" seam. Leave open between marks.

E. Trim seams, especially the batting. Clip edges, the bottom point and the top center. Turn right side out. Stitch opening closed.

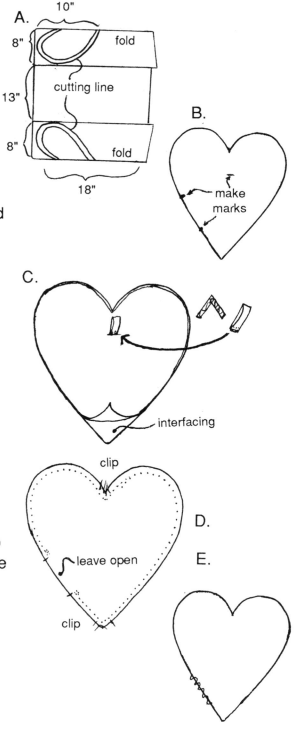

WALLHANGING - HEARTS Continued

DESIGN 2 - Two Tone Heart

-materials listed above PLUS
-1/2" yard of coordinate fabric or 12"
   square of left-over fabric
-tear-away interfacing

A.

Two Color Heart - Layout and Cut

A. Cut out hearts as stated above in Step A and B. Cut the smaller heart from a coordinate fabric.

Applique

B. Mark where the coordinate heart is to be placed, then use a fabric glue stick to place the coordinate heart in place. Place tear-away interfacing to the wrong side of the large front heart.

C. Stitch around the design to keep it in place. Then use a close together medium wide satin zig zag stitch to finish around the design. The closer the stitches are together the richer the finished look.

Assemble

D. As stated above in Steps C - F.

Variation 1: Three color heart.
Cut out a medium heart from a second color and a small heart from a third color. Satin stitch around each heart.

Variation 2: Cut out your childs initials or the letters **L-O-V-E** and applique one on each heart.

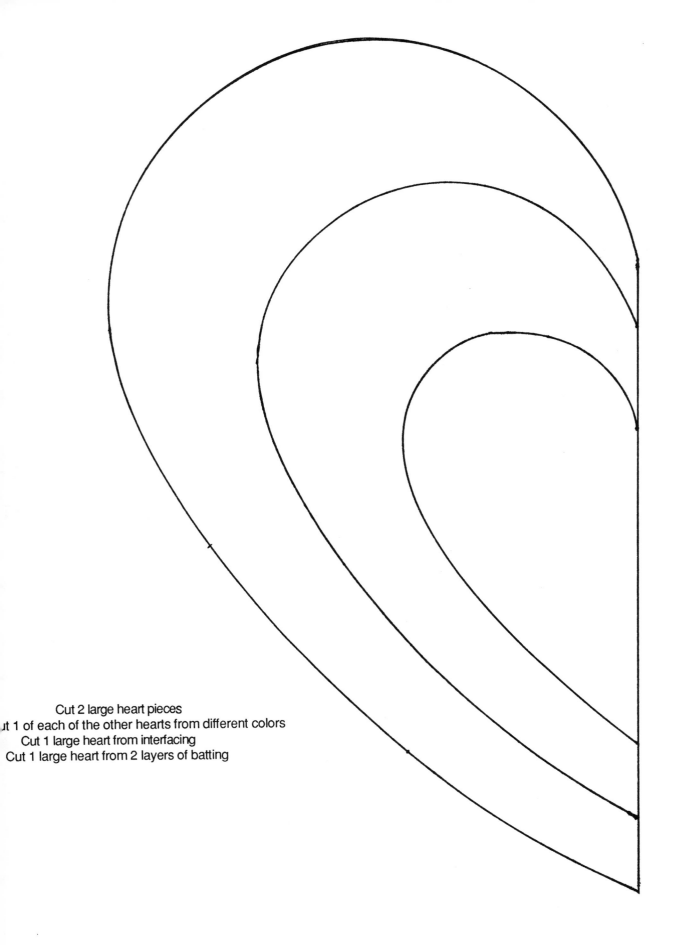

Cut 2 large heart pieces
Cut 1 of each of the other hearts from different colors
Cut 1 large heart from interfacing
Cut 1 large heart from 2 layers of batting

BLOCKS

For each 6" block you need:
-1/4 yard 45" fabric **OR**
  Six 7" squares from fabric of your choice
-polyester fiberfill

Layout and Cut

A. Cut six 7" squares.

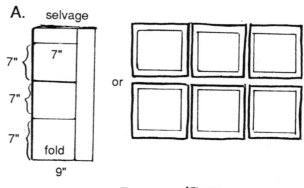

Sewing Directions - Block Strip

B. Take two squares, lay them right sides together. Stitch 1/2" seam on one side.

C. Open squares. Lay another square right sides together with one of the attached squares. Stitch 1/2" seam along opposite edge of square so you will have three in a row. Continue until you have four in a row.

Assembling

D. Fold the four squares in half (two facing two) with right sides together. Stitch 1/2" seam connecting all four, making a circle.

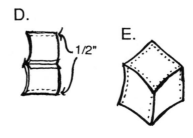

E. Take fifth square. Place it right sides together with one of the connected squares. Pin the four squares around it matching corners to seams then stitch 1/2" seam, easing the fabric in around the corners.

F. Pin the last square the same as above stitch three sides leaving fourth side open.

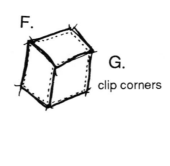

G. Clip corners and turn right side out.

H. Fill with fiberfill.

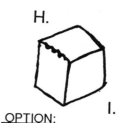

I. Stitch last side closed.

OPTION: Applique a small design on one, two or all six sides.

CUDDLEY

Make the top of the Cuddley from one of the bear, bunny, cat, dog, duck, lion or mouse Diaper Toppers. For the bottom portion you will need the following materials:

-1/2 yard of a soft fabric, fake fur, terry cloth, velveteen or satin
-5 feet of 1/2" wide double fold bias tape, fabric tape, or my kids like the satin blanket binding.

NOTE: This could also help solve the problem of what to do with your child's favorite blanket that is full of holes. Cut a portion of the blanket with the least number of holes.

open

Layout and Cut - Edges

A. Cut out a 14" square from fabric or blanket.

B. Pin tape around the fabric piece folding fabric at the corners. Stitch close to inside edge.

A.

14"

14"

B.

1/4"

Assembling

C. Fold fabric or blanket into a cone shape by folding opposite corners in to meet in the middle of the panel.

D. Place top of blanket 3" to the inside of the diaper topper opening.

E. Stitch opening closed.

Variation:

Turn under 1/4" and 1/4" on all edges, stitch close to inside edge.

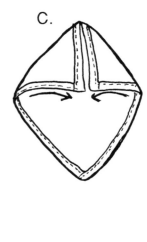

D.

C.

E.

MOBILES

These mobiles are designed with baby in mind. Designs will hang so baby sees the shape rather than Mom and Dad.

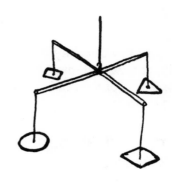

-felt pieces large enough to cut two of each
   object you want to make **OR**
-1/4 yard of fabric will make all items
   from the same fabric
-batting may be used
-interfacing

Layout and Cut - From Felt

A. Trace your designs from the page onto tracing paper then cut them out from the paper.

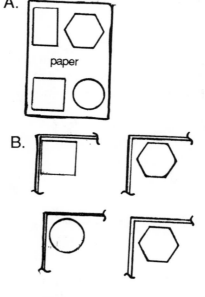

B. Lay design on top of two layers of felt. Trace around the design with fabric marker or chalk. Cut out along the line. Mark center dot on back of each design to attach hanging thread.

C. To give shape and support to object, cut designs from two layers of quilt batting and one layer of interfacing. Cut batting and interfacing 1/4" smaller than the pattern.

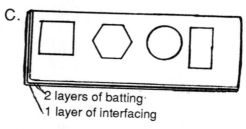

2 layers of batting·
1 layer of interfacing

Sewing Directions

D. Place batting and interfacing between felt pieces. Stitch close to edge on all sides.

To Hang See Step H page 109

Layout and Cut - From Fabric

E. Lay design on top of two layers of fabric. Cut object 1/4" larger than your design. Cut each design from two layers of quilt batting and one from interfacing.

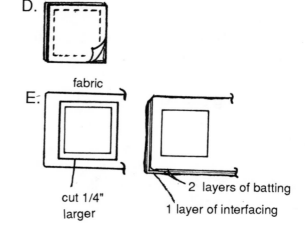

fabric

cut 1/4"
larger

2 layers of batting
1 layer of interfacing

F. Place fabric pieces right sides together with interfacing on the top and batting on the bottom. Stitch 1/4" seam around design leaving 2" open in the middle of one side to turn right side out. Clip corners and trim away batting.

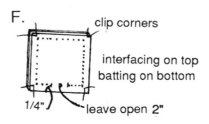

F.

clip corners

interfacing on top
batting on bottom

1/4" leave open 2"

G. Turn right side out. Hand stitch opening closed.

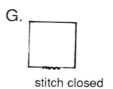

G.

stitch closed

Hanging Thread

H. Use 24" of heavy duty thread, use it as a double thread so the stitching length will be 12" long. Tie a knot in the end and pull it through the hanging mark until the knot is to the back side of the object. Cut the mid-point of the thread at the needle, remove needle, and tie the threads into a knot.

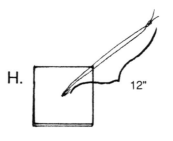

H.

12"

Hanging Design

I. Use two 18"x5/16" dowels. Mark center point on each dowel. Position dowels so 9" marks are on top of each other and perpendicular to each other. Hammer a nail through both dowels; nail head will be at the bottom. Bend remainder of nail to make a hook to hang from ceiling **OR** purchase a mobile arm that attaches to the crib.

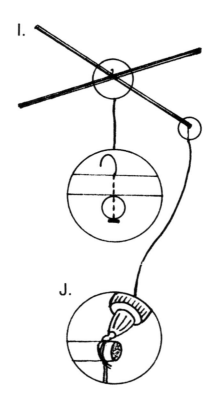

I.

J. Place the knot over the dowel. Wrap the thread around the dowel several times and glue it in place.

J.

Variation:

Make one of the shapes from fabric or terrycloth.
Fill with fiberfil to use as a baby teether.

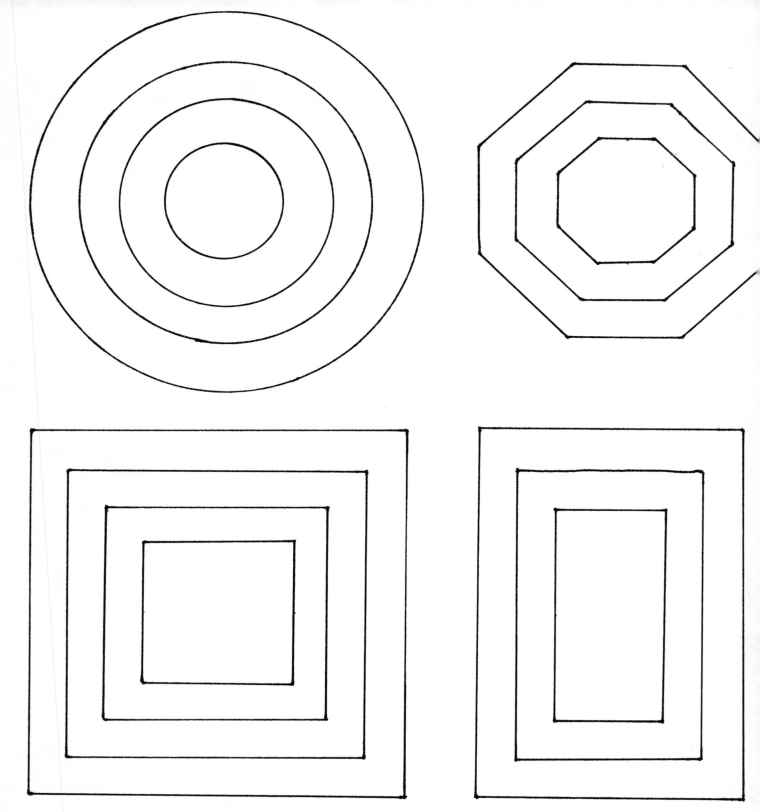

Cut 2 of each shape from fabric or felt
(1/4" larger if from fabric)
Cut 1 of each shape from interfacing

Make mobile of one shape with different sizes or of different
shapes.

Make mobile of one shape with different sizes or of different shapes.

Cut 2 of each shape from fabric or felt
(1/4" larger if from fabric)
Cut 1 of each shape from interfacing

Cut 2 of each shape from fabric or felt
(1/4" larger if from fabric)
Cut 1 of each shape from interfacing

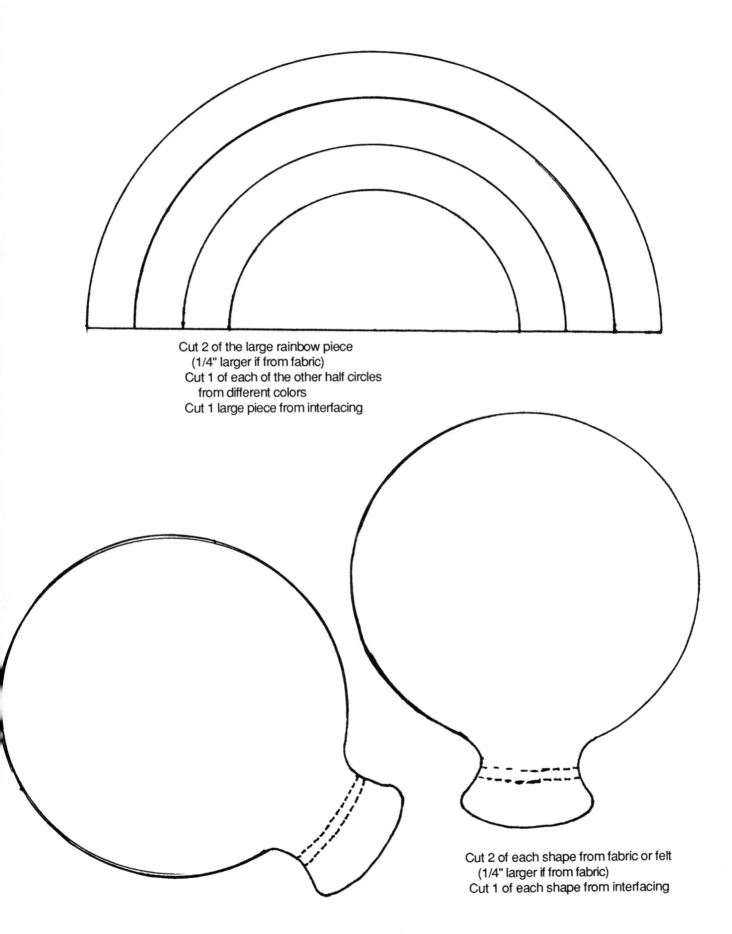

Cut 2 of the large rainbow piece
   (1/4" larger if from fabric)
Cut 1 of each of the other half circles
   from different colors
Cut 1 large piece from interfacing

Cut 2 of each shape from fabric or felt
   (1/4" larger if from fabric)
Cut 1 of each shape from interfacing

CHANGING TABLE AND NURSERY SAFETY

You plan where the baby will sleep, so take some time to plan and organize where you will change him.

First decide where to change the baby. Have a surface about waist high to avoid bending over to prevent lower back strain. Use a crib, a changing table or convert a dresser top to a changing area. Make this a piece of furniture that will also store clothes so you won't have to walk across the room to get a change of clothes.

Place the diaper stacker up on the wall with the diapers in it. It will be most convenient if the stacker is between the changing table and the crib.

Cover the surface with a towel or a changing table pad and cover*.
Place a catch-all* over the changing table. Put ointments, cornstarch, wet wipes, shoes and TOYS in the pockets. Why toys? They will hold the childs attention while you are changing his diapers, helping to keep him still and not squirming around. You will have more control of the baby, preventing him from falling from the changing table and avoiding injury. Plus, it is easier for you to have everything in one place.

Why organize the changing area? So you will NEVER have to leave the baby on top of the changing table while you go get clothes, wipes, ointments or powders. Never leave your baby on the changing area while you go get something or answer the telephone. Take the baby with you or put him in the crib.

Nursery Safety Tips

Check Electrical cords - try and place them behind furniture. When children start crawling they can pull the cords and pull fixtures onto them.

Check Electrical Outlets - place childproof plugs in them so they won't be able to stick keys, hangers or anything else into the outlet.

Windows - Make sure windows have secure latches. Have screens on the windows BUT, remember, they are not protection to keep a child from falling out.

Toys - You have heard most of this before but it is worth repeating. Keep toys with sharp corners or small pieces away from your child. Avoid toys with small pieces that will come off easily and get swallowed.

If you put toys on shelves, make sure they are sturdy and won't fall over if the child tries to climb. Keep toys on lower shelves. If you have toys too high the child may try to climb for them and pull the shelves over. If there are toys you don't want played with unless you are around, put them away where they can't be seen.

Toy Chests - Wooden boxes with heavy lids are dangerous unless there is a safety hinge that can be locked to keep it open while the child is playing.

Trunks with latch front closures should be avoided. The child could close himself in the box and not be able to get out. Children like to hide so make sure he can't get inside and not be able to get out.

The plastic containers or wood boxes with sliding tops are fine. Many of the wooden ones have the book shelves above which are really handy.

MONEY SAVER TIPS

Instead of buying 45" Fabric
Buy a child's sheet or double flat sheet. You can buy one for about $6.00 and make many of these items from one sheet.

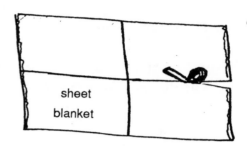

Instead of Flannel
Use a sheet blanket. A full size blanket can be purchased for around $5.00 and can make one baby comforter and two receiving blankets or four single thickness receiving blankets that are a real nice size.

sheet blanket

Instead of Bias Tape
Make your own tape from fabric. For these items, it is not necessary to use the bias.
A. Cut 2 " strips as long as you need.
B. Press strip in half lengthwise.
C. Open out, press sides in to meet at center.
D. Fold on original fold.

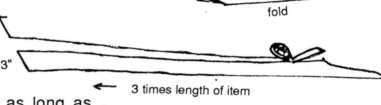

A. 2"

B. fold

C. fold fold

D. fold

E.

Instead of Rick Rack
Use ruffle made from fabric.
E. Cut 3" wide strip three times as long as the item is around.

3" ← 3 times length of item

F. Press it in half lengthwise and machine baste two lines of stitching 1/8" and 1/4" from raw edge. Pull bottom threads to gather.

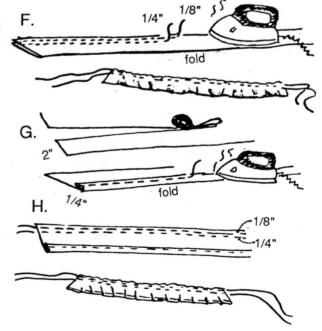

F. 1/4" 1/8" fold

OR
G. Cut 2" strip three times as long as you need. Press under 1/4" and 1/4" again on one edge. Stitch 1/8" from inside edge.

G. 2" 1/4" fold

H. Gather opposite edge by stitching 1/8" and 1/4" from raw edge. Pull bottom threads. Place ruffle in unstitched seam.

H. 1/8" 1/4"

SHOWER IDEAS

Dimmer Switch

A small basket lined with a receiving blanket and filled with small bottles of lotion, shampoo, baby cornstarch, soap and oil to be used in the diaper bag.

Sleepers with snaps down BOTH legs.

Infant front pack.

One piece jump-suits for baby.

Self-made cloth picture frame or the pewter/gold frame with the babies birth weight, length, date and time of birth.

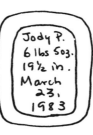

Silverware for the child.

Silverplate rattle (feels good on the gums when teething and won't crack or break.)

Decopage wall plaque with birth information and Friday's child phrase.

Toddler Bath Towel with applique name and/or design.

Other Suggestions:
Don't buy newborn size clothes unless the gift is given immediately and if the child is very small (5 lbs at birth).

Becareful giving summer clothes for the child to grow into them (sunsuits, swimsuits). By the time the child grows into them it might be winter.

Also, don't forget Mom. It's nice to give a little something to Mom. Earrings, perfume, bubble bath, or night gown. It may help ease the after baby blues.

INDEX

CAR SEAT TOY BAG

-3/8 yard 45" fabric
-11" of 1/4" elastic
-2 velcro tabs

Layout and Cut

A.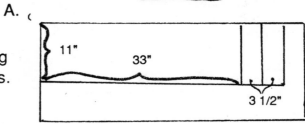

A. Cut one piece of fabric 11"x33" for bag panel and two pieces 3 1/2"x11" for sides.

Sewing Directions -
Sides Panels

B.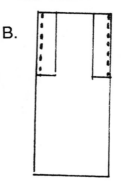

B. Take side panels and place them right sides together so 3 1/2" sides are even with 11" side of bag panel. Stitch 1/2" seam along side. Zig zag edge.

Casing

C.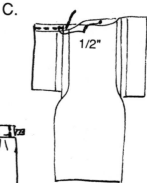

C. On top edge, turn under 1/2" and 1/2" again. Topstitch 1/8" from inside edge making a casing.

D.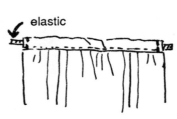

D. Push 11" of elastic through casing opening. Stitch elastic in place at side openings.

Side Seams

E.

E. Stitch 1/2" seam across bottom and up other side, easing corners of side strip.

Finishing

F.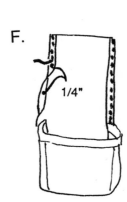

F. Turn under 1/4" and 1/4" again on top side of remaining fabric. Topstitch 1/8" from inside edge.